THE IDIOM OF POETRY

THE IDIOM

OF POETRY

By Frederick A. Pottle

REVISED EDITION, WITH OTHER ESSAYS

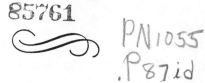

Bloomington

Indiana University Press

1963

This book in its original form consisted of six lectures delivered at Cornell University in the spring of 1941, namely, the Messenger Lectures on the Evolution of Civilization, a series founded in 1923 under the terms of the will of Hiram J. Messenger, B. Litt., Ph.D., of Hartford, Connecticut. Chapters VII, VIII, and IX were added in the second (1946) edition. Chapter VII was delivered as one of the Averill Lectures at Colby College in 1942. Chapter VIII, originally a paper read in 1936 at the Clergy Conference of the Diocese of New York, was enlarged and printed in 1938 in a collection entitled *Affirmations;* it was reprinted, after some revision, with the permission of Messrs. Sheed and Ward, the publishers, and Canon Bernard Iddings Bell, the editor of the volume. Chapter IX was a paper read to the Clergy Conference of the Diocese of New York in 1943.

Copyright 1946 by Cornell University
Copyright © 1963 by Indiana University Press

Second edition, revised and enlarged

Midland Book edition 1963 by arrangement with
Cornell University Press

Manufactured in the United States of America

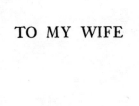
TO MY WIFE

FROM THE
PREFACE TO THE SECOND EDITION

It is the fate of any man who advances a relativistic argument like that developed in this book to produce a more vigorous reaction than the occasion, coolly considered, seems to warrant. The reason is that all relativistic arguments clash with attitudes which some one or other holds as a matter of faith. The Great Enlightenment went very far to weaken faith in historical religions, but it did nothing whatever to lessen the amount of orthodoxy: it only gave us more questionable varieties. Every man, without any exception, has his orthodoxies, or at least one orthodoxy. With a very large number of people today the orthodoxy is political or nationalist. With many it is racial. Some men are dogmatic purists. I once knew a very great man who was an orthographic absolutist; tolerant even to a fault in everything else, he had real difficulty in keeping his temper when any one advocated even the mildest forms of simplified spelling. An alarming number of people today, as it seems to me, demonstrate in connection with literature a fervor, a dogmatic certainty, a fanatical exclusiveness, which has all the marks of displaced religion. I am all for orthodoxy, but it is my belief that the only safe and proper area for orthodoxy is in faith and morals, and that religious orthodoxy—for its own sake—should be pretty strictly limited to that portion of belief which is guaranteed by revelation.

F. A. P.

PREFACE TO MIDLAND BOOK EDITION

W<small>HEN</small> *The Idiom of Poetry* went out of print some years ago, I did not raise my voice in protest; I assumed that re-printing meant revision, and I was reluctant to confront myself in that book again. Then last year I came on the preface that Violet Paget ("Vernon Lee") wrote in 1906 for a re-issue of her *Studies of the Eighteenth Century in Italy*, and thought the thing might be tolerable if I could handle matters as she did. When the proposal for the present edition unexpectedly came, I got that preface out and read it again. It still seemed to me so satisfactory that I decided simply to lift her first paragraph, changing only a word here and there to fit it completely to my needs.

"I have not attempted to revise this new edition of my old book; I have even resisted the curiosity of knowing what it was like—at least how it would strike me after twenty years. For to revise would be to criticize; to criticize would be to demolish; and having demolished these essays, I should be unable to rebuild them. First of all, and odd though it may sound, I no longer possess enough knowledge to judge, let alone correct them, from the theoretical point of view; and my suspicion of their being (despite the deference still occasionally paid to them) plentifully garnished with pertness and naïveté, is, so to speak, *a priori* and due to knowledge of the author rather than to any further lights on the subject. On the contrary, I am aware of growing darkness on all matters touching theory of poetry and theology. This feeling has been a chief reason for refusing to revise, or rather to re-read, my old book. The other reason is more subtle but even more cogent: I have noticed that the work of young writers is not only much worse but unluckily at times much less bad than that of the elders and betters they grow into. No writer can distinguish between self-satisfaction and satisfactory work, still less be sure that what he takes for mature judgment and more delicate taste is not the *jejeune* beginning of old age. We think we are more estimable, perhaps even more agreeable, than we were when we were younger; meanwhile we notice that the wits and spirits, as well as the figures and complexions, of our contemporaries have not always improved. My *Idiom of Poetry* must be brimful of presumptuousness and naïveté; but had the author been less naïve and presumptuous, the book would perhaps not have been written and certainly would not have been so deserving of being read. Thanks to its enthusiasm and ruthlessness, it may possess some small value. And because I think so, I have refused to lay indifferent hands, and even skeptical eyes, upon it."

I suppose I would have revised it if I had thought that it was really so hard to follow as the continuing misconceptions of what I tried to say would seem to indicate. But whatever the defects of *The Idiom of Poetry*, I cannot honestly convince myself that they include obscurity and inconsistency. Do what he may, the critical relativist presents doctrine so novel to the literary mind that he is bound to be attacked without being apprehended and answered without being read. I shall simply repeat that I have never said nor implied that there are no objective standards of criticism, or that any age ever lacks such standards. I have never said nor implied that we should build watertight compartments for periods of poetry and never judge poetry except by the standards of the times that produced it. What I have said is that the standards for judging poetry change and should change; and that though we properly grant privileged status to our own standards, history will withdraw the privilege.

I have, of course, thought of strategies I might employ if I were writing a wholly new book. I should, I think, play down subjectivism and merely physiological determinism, and should develop the concept of "mental climate," making "mental climate" coordinate with "sensibility" and "idiom." I should present shifts of sensibility as resulting from changes in the climate of opinion; or rather, should lay out "climate of opinion," "sensibility," and "idiom" in a causally related series having a general drift from left to right but with concurrent reaction in the reverse direction.

I should introduce early, and make continuing use of, Ferdinand de Saussure's terms "synchronical" and "diachronical" to designate the two axes of critical approach that I discern and recommend. I don't like special terminology, and in discourse so deliberately popular as *The Idiom of Poetry* such terms are bound to seem jargon, but special terminology does force readers to notice that distinctions are being made, or at least attempted.

I should use the term "objective" oftener, and might even

question whether some writers who make confident use of the term "absolute" really mean any more than "objective." And I should try to demonstrate that the objectively based norms of meaning that are held to testify to the "existence" of a poem do not provide us with an entity like a surd number (which never "comes out even" no matter how far you carry the decimals to the right) or the planet Mars seen through the obscuring and distorting haze of the earth's atmosphere. They provide, not a determinate object that we can approximate, but statistical limits to varied and sometimes opposed meanings.

If the human race were wiped out (no extravagant supposition these days), the objective possibilities for physical science would remain just what they are now. If the ants or the bees awoke to science, their symbolic notations would be such as we cannot even imagine, but their science would be identical with ours. If, on the other hand, the human race were wiped out, what we call poetry would be gone for ever. Formic or apian art would not in the least resemble human art. Science explores a nature that could go on existing without a human being in the universe; poetry explores that aspect of specifically human nature that I have called sensibility. The science of an era does not explore nature impartially and in all directions: each age makes the excursions that interest it most, and what is interesting is determined by the climate of opinion. So, too, with poetry. The periods of poetry explore congenial areas of human sensibility, and it sometimes happens that the areas preferred by successive periods have little overlap. Furthermore, in the country of poetry, unlike the country of the scientists, surface change is constant and of the utmost significance. But though the possibilities for exploration are practicably inexhaustible, there is no reason to suppose that the country is infinite in extent. There, I suppose, is something like an absolute: the sum of all the possibilities of exploration. But we can know only what has been explored and can make no safe guesses about what lies beyond the frontiers. We are concerned that the explorers shall not have confused mirages with lands actually seen, but we shall not expect explorers of different areas to have seen the same things.

So, though I should be glad to clear myself of imputations of facile radicalism adopted for mere shock value, I remain a critical relativist. What I have set myself against is fundamentally, I suppose, Wordsworth's disparaging dictum that the poetry of all ages is *stained* with the peculiarities of its age. Historicity, I assert, is not a stain in or on literature; it is constitutive, of its essence. It is not like red ink splashed in water or on cloth; it is rather like red light in light prevailingly red, a nonreducible characteristic wave length. And the notion that *we* somehow escape historicity is an illusion. The present is part of history.

F. A. P.

New Haven, Connecticut
  April 2, 1963

CONTENTS

THE IDIOM OF POETRY

"IF, IN WHAT I am about to say, it shall appear to some that my labour is unnecessary, and that I am like a man fighting a battle without enemies, such persons may be reminded that, whatever be the language outwardly holden by men, a practical faith in the opinions which I am wishing to establish is almost unknown."—WORDSWORTH, Preface to the *Lyrical Ballads* (1800).

I

SHIFTS OF SENSIBILITY

I HAVE often thought that it would be good sense as well as good manners if, at the very beginning of such a series as this, the lecturer and his audience drew up a contract setting forth what was to be expected on both sides. In the spirit of such a contract, I offer the following articles:

1) These lectures will deal with theory of poetry and theory of criticism. Except for a bit of the fifth lecture and the greater part of the sixth, which will be an attempt to apply some of the principles of the preceding discourses, they will not interpret or criticize any particular poetry. In general my statements will have about the same relation to poetry that a botany textbook has to flowers.

2) My approach will be "psychological" rather than "philosophical"; that is, I shall deal more with mechanism than with spirit. Poems I shall define in terms of communication and the effect they produce on us, not in terms of what is called realist philosophy, which regards them as determinate things, having an existence apart from a particular perceiving mind. I promise to avoid special terminology and all metaphysics that are not common property. I think I shall be understandable throughout.

3) I do not consider the psychological or mechanistic approach exclusive. I am one of those persons, annoying both to materialists and to idealists, who see no intellectual or moral depravity in being both on occasion: that is, in studying matters of this sort sometimes as mechanism, sometimes as mind controlling or constructing mechanism. I regard the methods of science and the methods of theology as both valid, but as discontinuous: that is, I find each logically consistent within its own assumptions, but I do not find it possible to harmonize them in one logically coherent system. The scientific or naturalistic method, if it is not to be vitiated at the start, must be kept rigorously free from all appeal to knowledge not referable to sensory experience or not capable, in theory at least, of experimental verification. Theology assumes cosmic purposiveness, absolutes of various kinds, the validity of non-sensory experience, and may base itself on truths which it considers revealed. All of us are agreed practically that the naturalistic method *must* be the one chosen to resolve the majority of our daily problems. The man who aims a gun or builds a bridge or designs an airplane is a scientist; but so also is a man who plants a garden or a woman who bakes a cake. Yet the scientific method is by no means limited to this area where it reigns by necessity. It can be applied to any human problem whatsoever: that is, it can be expected to give some kind of answer under any possible set of circumstances. The limitation of science about which we hear so much is not that when faced with certain questions it has nothing to say; it is rather that its answers appear to be of little or no utility. And if we are honest, we shall have to say the same of theology. Our practical lives, however much we may try

2

to conceal the fact from ourselves, are a tangle of efforts to decide whether we shall proceed from naturalistic or supernaturalistic assumptions, whether we shall be scientists or theologians. I accept this state of affairs as an inevitable consequence of the finite nature of the mind of man, and turn without any sense of shame from one system to the other as circumstances, after serious trial, seem to warrant. I do not brand as "false" any logically coherent system of thought because I have found it less satisfactory than another for handling a particular problem. I simply try to decide, in each application, which system *works* best, that is, which illuminates the greater number of facts. It is my contention that no theory of poetry is satisfactory unless it makes sense out of history. And the conclusion I have come to, and shall develop in these lectures, is that we can make better sense out of history if we recognize *two* values in poetry, an aesthetic value and a moral value; and that we can get better results if we approach the first through a naturalistic system and the second through a theological.

It would not be proper for me to write the articles on your side of the agreement, but if it were proper, I should suggest something like the following:

1) You will not expect from these discourses the pleasure proper to poetry, nor even a reflection of that pleasure. I shall not compose poetry, and shall interpret and criticize poetry only at the very end of the series. I am dealing with *theory* of poetry, an abstract, intellectual thing; and if what I say rouses any excitement at all, it will be of the rational intellect, not of the emotions.

2) Since I shall refrain from esoteric metaphysics and

3

technical vocabulary, you will permit me to be "popular" and hazy, rather than precise and obscure. You will be kind enough to suppose that I know a good many hard words, and that I could have used them if I had thought this was the occasion for such a display.

3) The third article on my side of the contract will involve me in a tiresome amount of paraphrase and qualification. If I cannot say that anybody's theory of poetry is "wrong" or "false," and must always call it "less illuminating" or "less useful" or "less inclusive," I shall be divesting myself of some of the most powerful weapons of persuasion. You will allow your admiration for my candor to cancel your annoyance at my inconclusiveness. Most important of all, you will agree not to criticize me for not saying things that would be proper for a mystical theory of poetry, but wholly out of place in the framework which I have chosen. If you consider that there is no utility in my scheme, you will repudiate it entire by staying away after this lecture. You may suppose that I know enough about mystical aesthetic to be able to frame hypotheses in that vocabulary, and to state the solutions offered by that aesthetic to the problems which I shall handle. If I am as careful as I hope to be, these lectures will provide few collisions between the two systems.

When a critic, great or humble, says that a poem is good or bad, what is he doing? When, of two equally respectable contemporary critics, one labels a given work good and the other says it is a failure, what has happened? When the best critics of one age repudiate the darling of the best critics of a preceding generation, what are we

4

to think? Or, to put the questions concretely: When Messrs. Brooks and Warren say that Shelley's *Indian Serenade* is a bad poem, how do they know? Poe calls it "exquisite," Browning thought it "divine." When T. S. Eliot and Paul Elmer More disagree about the value of Joyce's *Ulysses*, what is the cause of the disagreement? When Matthew Arnold and A. E. Housman pass judgments on Dryden diametrically opposed to those of Johnson and Gray, how shall we account for it? The history of criticism is a tangle of such conflicts.

A great many explanations could be advanced, but they would all be found upon examination to be different combinations of two factors: standard or measure, and ability of the critic using it. Messrs. Brooks and Warren applied some kind of standard to Shelley's poem and found the poem wanting. Eliot and More each applied a measure to *Ulysses*. Arnold and Housman remeasured Dryden after he had been measured by Johnson and Gray. There are three, and I think only three, ways of accounting for the discrepancies. We can suppose that the measure used by all these critics was accurate, in which case we must conclude that either Eliot or More, either Johnson or Housman, was inexpert in applying it. Or we can suppose that the ability in all these cases was about the same, but that one set of critics had a grossly inaccurate measure, while the other had one certified by some critical Bureau of Standards. Or we can suppose that the measure in all cases was a variable, and a variable of a particularly distressing kind; that it had a habit of contracting or expanding without revealing the fact. Either the first or the second of these positions is the one usually taken, and of course they

5

do account satisfactorily for many of the vagaries of criticism. But I shall defend the third, which is the position of critical relativism. That is, I shall maintain that all critical judgments are relative to the age producing them, since the measure or standard varies unpredictably from one age to another. By this system, Johnson and Housman were wrong only in asserting absolute judgments. Each was right so far as he reported honestly the result of the application of his measure.

During the last twenty-five years a good deal has been said about measures that expand and contract. Most of us, I fancy, first got the disquieting news from Sir Arthur Eddington's brilliant popularization, *The Nature of the Physical World*, which I shall draw upon—I hope in decent paraphrase—in what follows. The news is really much older than twenty-five years. Before the turn of this century it had been demonstrated experimentally and verified theoretically that any moving measuring rod, no matter what the material of which it is composed, contracts when it is turned parallel to its line of motion, and expands when it is turned across that line. And all measuring rods on this earth are moving. Any given spot on the earth's surface is wheeling about the earth's axis at a speed of something like a quarter of a mile a second, and around the sun at a speed of about nineteen. One might hastily conclude from this that our measuring rods are fairly constant in length when they lie north and south, but that when lying east and west they alternately expand and contract as the earth's rotation brings them across or in line with the direction of its orbital motion. Then, after a little figuring, one might triumphantly announce that by the physicists' own figures, the variations in length of an object moving less than twenty miles a second are inconsiderable, even on the scientific scale.

I say we should be hasty if we drew that conclusion, because matters are by no means so simple as that. In making the statement we assumed that the sun was stationary, and that the spot of earth on which the measuring rod lies had only the two velocities of rotation around the earth's axis and of revolution around the sun. As a matter of fact, the sun appears not to be stationary: our solar system seems to be drifting toward a point in the constellation Hercules. And the entire galaxy of which the solar system is a part may be moving with terrific velocity—a velocity which would make the contraction of our measuring rods far from inconsiderable. This is not one of the unsolved problems of science to which posterity will find the answer. It is something we shall never be able to find out. We can, it is true, chart a relative displacement between our system and bodies outside our galaxy, but that will not enable us to determine the rate of movement of our system. Suppose we do observe a nebula that, as we say, is receding from the earth at the rate of one thousand miles a second. At such a speed the variation of measuring rods would be quite appreciable in laboratory measurements. If the earth were hurtling through space at that rate, and we wished our measurements to be accurate in any absolute sense, it would be necessary to make corrections for position of the measuring rod or scale. And the earth *may* be moving at that rate. All we have really observed is that the earth and the nebula are getting farther apart. Actually it may be the nebula that is standing still

7

and the earth that is receding. Suppose I stop paraphrasing Eddington, and quote him directly:

> "There is no means of deciding . . . to which of us the observed relative velocity of 1000 miles a second *really* belongs. Astronomically the galaxy of which the earth is a member does not seem to be more important, more central, than the nebula. The presumption that it is we who are the more nearly at rest has no serious foundation; it is mere self-flattery."

The result of such speculation was the breakdown of classical physics, which was based upon a calm conviction of the absolute nature of scientific measurements. Ordinary scales might be inaccurate, but the scale of a scientist was accurate. His steel measure, of course, would vary slightly in length with changes of temperature, but he was aware of the change and could apply the proper correction. Now the bottom is dropped from under him. All his measurements, it appears, are merely relative to his rate of motion, and he does not know what his rate of motion is. He has, to use the accepted terminology, a "frame of space" to which he must refer all his observations as to position and volume. An observer on another planet having a different velocity has a different frame of space. Common sense tells us urgently that *our* frame of space is unique, absolute, "real"; but that, as Eddington said, is only self-flattery. Let us continue the quotation:

> "Einstein's theory is that the question of a unique right frame of space does not arise. There is a frame of space *relative* to a terrestrial observer, another frame *relative* to the nebular observers, others *relative* to other

stars. Frames of space are relative. Distances, lengths, volumes—all quantities of space-reckoning which belong to the frames—are likewise relative. A distance as reckoned by an observer on one star is as good as the distance reckoned by an observer on another star. We must not expect them to agree; the one is a distance relative to one frame, the other is a distance relative to another frame. *Absolute distance, not relative to some special frame, is meaningless.*"

There is a very stubborn tendency of the human mind, after reading paragraphs like these, to persist in denying the conclusion by resorting to the expressed or unexpressed theory of *illusion*. (Things may *seem* so and so to given observers, but they are *really* otherwise.) Einstein has given a classical illustration of relativity which will show what I mean. Suppose a bomber in the air and an observer stationary on the earth. The bombardier releases his bomb some distance from the target. Let us ignore the effect of air resistance on the bomb (which of course a real bombardier cannot do), and assume furthermore that the plane maintains the same velocity which it had when the bomb was released. The observer on the ground will see the bomb descend in a long parabolic curve. The bombardier will see the bomb go down in a straight line. Neither is under the slightest illusion. The path of the bomb relative to the earth *is* a parabolic curve; the path relative to the moving plane *is* a straight line. There is no reason for assuming that either is more "real" than the other. If you are bothered by the concept of simultaneous differing realities, your only resource is a description which will combine the relations of both: that is, one which will show the relation of the bomb, at each moment of its flight, to *both* the earth and the plane.

Literary criticism seems always to have resembled "classical" physics. From the time of Aristotle to the present day, critics must have believed in the possibility of absolute judgments, for they have always been making them. Would it not be well, with the example of the scientists before us, if we looked at the critics' standard or measure to assure ourselves that it is an unchanging scale, or, if it varies, that the variations are of a kind that can be predicted and allowed for? The material for such an investigation is almost unlimited, for wherever any one has recorded a literary judgment, there is stuff to our hand. Any literary judgments will do. But I do not know a better lot for our purpose than those passed generally on the poetry of the eighteenth century by the Romantic and Victorian poets: Wordsworth, Arnold, A. E. Housman. Suppose I choose Housman as a spokesman. His judgments are just the same as Wordsworth's or Arnold's, but the modern instance is rather more pungent. The extract that follows is pretty long, but I want to make sure that I have played fair in stating the position which I wish to attack. And none of you will object to the relief furnished by an interlude of really good prose.

"There is also such a thing as sham poetry, a counterfeit deliberately manufactured and offered as a substitute. In English the great historical example is certain verse produced abundantly and applauded by high and low in what for literary purposes is loosely called the eighteenth century: not a hundred years accidentally begun and ended by chronology, but a longer period which is a unity and a reality; the period lying between *Samson Agonistes* in 1671 and the *Lyrical Ballads* in 1798, and including as an integral part and indeed as its most potent influence the mature work of Dryden. . . .

"There has now for a good many years been a strong disposition to revise the verdict pronounced by the nineteenth century on the poetry of the eighteenth and to represent that its disparaging judgment was no more than an expression of distaste for a sort of poetry unlike its own. That is a misconception. It set a low value on the poetry of the eighteenth century, not because it differed in kind from its own, but because, even at its best, it differed in quality, as its own best poetry did not differ, from the poetry of all those ages, whether modern or ancient, English or foreign, which are acknowledged as the great ages of poetry. . . .

"The human faculty which dominated the eighteenth century and informed its literature was the intelligence, and that involved, as Arnold says, 'some repressing and silencing of poetry,' 'some touch of frost to the imaginative life of the soul.' Man had ceased to live from the depths of his nature; he occupied himself for choice with thoughts which do not range beyond the sphere of the understanding. . . .

"To poets of the eighteenth century high and impassioned poetry did not come spontaneously, because the feelings which foster its birth were not then abundant and urgent in the inner man; but they girt up their loins and essayed a lofty strain at the bidding of ambition. The way to write real poetry, they thought, must be to write something as little like prose as possible;

they devised for the purpose what was called a 'correct and splendid diction,' which consisted in always using the wrong word instead of the right, and plastered it as ornament, with no thought of propriety, on whatever they desired to dignify. . . . A thick, stiff, unaccommodating medium was interposed between the writer and his work. And this deadening of language had a consequence beyond its own sphere: its effect worked inward, and deadened perception. That which could no longer be described was no longer noticed."

This is admirable. It gives, couched in a delightful style, a clear adverse critical judgment on the poetry of the eighteenth century, and it defines the measure or standard by which that judgment was arrived at. The verse of the eighteenth century, we are told, was in its essence not poetical. It was not poetical because during that period feeling was dominated by intellect. "Man had ceased to live from the depths of his nature." Though they had little or no poetry in them, the men of the eighteenth century still wanted the fame of poets, and to that end invented an artificial poetic diction. Matters got steadily worse, for the poetic diction progressively dried up whatever scanty springs of feeling the century had. And we can detect the anti-poetical character of eighteenth-century verse by a simple comparison or measurement. Eighteenth-century verse, "even at its best, differs in quality from the poetry of all those ages, whether modern or ancient, English or foreign, which are acknowledged as the great ages of poetry."

What could be more satisfactory? Have we not here a standard with the fixed, external, objective character that a standard ought to have? I think not; I should say that it was not objective at all. "The ages which are acknowledged"—by whom? By Mr. Housman and others of his sensibility. Is there any probability that critics who deny validity to the poetry of Pope will grant it to those works which his resemble, which were indeed his models? If the test were made genuinely historical—if it were stated in the form "all those poems which *have been* acknowledged as great poems"—it is exactly the test I should contend for. Our treasury of acknowledged masterpieces (acknowledged by some one or other at some time or other) is large and varied, and will provide precedents for the poetry of the eighteenth century, or, for that matter, for poetry of any kind whatever. The epistles of Horace; the satires of Horace, Juvenal, and Persius—during the greater part of literary history these have been ranked very high indeed. And I do not think it will be maintained that the more characteristic poetry of Pope differs in kind from theirs. In French poetry one could instance Malherbe, Boileau, and Voltaire, but it is unnecessary. The appeal to history, as made by Mr. Housman, is actually a subjective test.

And the subjective test is in fact admitted by him, and described by him more honestly and amusingly than by any one else:

"Poetry . . . seems to me more physical than intellectual. . . . Experience has taught me, when I am shaving of a morning, to keep watch over my thoughts, because, if a line of poetry strays into my memory, my skin bristles so that the razor ceases to act. This particular symptom is accompanied by a shiver down the spine; there is another which consists in a constriction of the throat and a precipitation of water to the eyes; and there is a third which I can only describe by borrowing a phrase from one of Keats's last letters, where he says, speaking of Fanny Brawne, 'everything that reminds me of her goes through me like a spear.' The seat of this sensation is the pit of the stomach."

Though I should hope that Mr. Housman, if challenged, would have stuck to his guns and maintained that every line that we honestly recognize as poetry causes a perceptible physiological disturbance, he would probably not have insisted that in all cases the disturbances must be as gross as those which he has described. Still, I think I shall be doing him no injustice if I say that his brilliant argument comes down to this: Real poetry makes a man's beard bristle, brings water into his eyes, and causes a constriction in the throat, tremors down the spine, and a sinking feeling in the pit of the stomach; eighteenth-century verse does not produce these effects on me, whence I infer that it never produced them on anybody. *Ergo*, the verse of the eighteenth century is not poetry.

The inference seems reasonable, but a scientist would challenge it instantly. He would wish to know whether Mr. Housman's affective mechanism was the same that men of the eighteenth century had. Outwardly it obviously was. Gross anatomy would have revealed no significant difference between Housman's nervous system and Pope's. That is not to answer the question. A telephone switchboard looks the same whether its plugs are in one set of holes or another, but the difference is enormous. A radio looks the same when its dial is set for one wave length as for another. Are we, in fact, very much like receiving sets, born into the world with clear reception in only one portion of the dial? I am sure that we are, and that consequently all our literary judgments are relative to our "set."

To demonstrate this most effectively, I ought to show that Dr. Johnson, when he read Pope, experienced as powerful feelings as Housman did when he read Blake, and that the feelings resulted from the same physiological disturbances which Housman has reported. I cannot do it, not because Johnson did not have the symptoms (I am sure he did), but because he would rather have died than write about them. It is amazing how few prominent critics have ever put themselves on record in that fashion. But it is not hard to show that men of the eighteenth century found plenty of feeling in Pope:

"Pope's knowledge was liberal and extensive; his genius was penetrating and ardent, and it was as rich, extensive, and various as his knowledge. We can hardly read a passage in that instructive, elegant, and harmonious—in that spirited, pathetick, and sublime—poet without very lively pleasure, or very forcible rapture. He no sooner invokes his Muse than she is perfectly propitious to his invocation: he informs and convinces; he exasperates; he soothes and melts us; he elevates and transports us, as the subject requires. . . .

"He was endowed with so feeling, so elegant, and ardent a soul; He was so eminently, so peculiarly qualified by nature to animate and adorn any object which He intended to exhibit with all the graces, that if He had only favoured the world with his translation of the *Iliad*, it would have ranked Him with our great and celebrated poets."

So wrote Dr. Johnson's friend Percival Stockdale, in *An Inquiry into the Nature and Genuine Laws of Poetry*, a work published in 1778. If you care to read that rather ridiculous book, you will find him on another page applying to Pope those very lines from Shakespeare ("The poet's eye, in a fine frenzy rolling," etc.) which the Romantic critics, almost to a man, have used to prove that Pope was not a poet. Byron, a violent partisan, maintained over and over that Pope was the greatest of English poets: "I was . . . mortified at the ineffable distance in point of sense, harmony, effect, and even *Imagination*, passion, and *Invention*, between the little Queen Anne's man, and us of the Lower Empire." Walter Scott said he had more pleasure in reading Johnson's *London* and *Vanity of Human Wishes* "than any other poetical composition he could mention," and remarks in his sketch of Johnson's life that "the deep and pathetic morality of *The Vanity of Human Wishes* has often extracted tears from those whose eyes wander dry over pages professedly sentimental." And James Ballantyne testified to the fact that Scott's features never showed a more lively play of expression than when he was reciting Johnson's poems.

Stockdale was a ridiculous man and, as I have said, wrote a rather ridiculous book. Byron was not a very good literary critic; he had many prejudices and was given to using criticism as a means of paying off personal grudges. But I do not know that we need to apologize in any way for Scott, who seems to have been as good a critic of literature, in an easygoing, non-theoretical way, as any man of his time. And after discounting heavily the remarks of Stockdale and Byron, one still has left the indubitable fact *that they found feeling—and intense feeling—in the poetry of the eighteenth century*. I say indubitable, for why should either have pretended to raptures which he did not feel?

Is it, on the face of it, reasonable to assume that Pope and his contemporaries had less feeling than the Romantics? What sort of conspiracy could have been so powerful that it kept men in general and poets in particular from *feeling* for a century or more? Poets are not so docile as that. Is it not fairly obvious that the total *quantity* of feeling—for obvious physiological reasons—is about the same from generation to generation? But surely I would not maintain that a rainbow or a waterfall excited as powerful feelings in Pope as in Wordsworth? Of course not. I would maintain that Pope had as much capacity for feeling as Wordsworth, but that his feelings were aroused by (or expressed by) different things. Since our own sensibility is organized in much the same fashion as Wordsworth's, we are largely incapacitated for feeling the poetry of Pope.

My basic objection to nearly all recorded criticism is that it assumes a fixed or absolute sensibility or basis of feeling: a natural, correct basis of feeling that all right men have had since the beginning of time, or that the critic has arrived at by special grace. The view I am propounding is that an absolute basis of feeling has no more existence than an absolute frame of space. All original criticism is subjective, being a report of the impact of the work upon the critic's sensibility; all criticism is relative to the critic's sensibility; and the question as to a "right" sensibility does not arise.

I find it useful to borrow from the science of linguistics the term *shift*, and to draw an analogy between the periods in literary history and the sound shifts in language. Every one, I suppose, has heard something about sound shifts, but not every one realizes how sudden (historically speaking) and mysterious those shifts were. During a given period in history, a period, let us say, embracing some centuries immediately preceding the Christian era, the parent Germanic language, which up to that time had preserved approximately the same consonant scheme as its sister tongues—Sanskrit, Latin, Greek, the Celtic group—suffered a thoroughgoing change. The sound represented by *p* became *f;* that represented by *t* became *th;* that represented by *k* became the sound written *ch* in German. Then *b, d, g* became *p, t, k*. The effect was almost totally to disguise the kinship of English, Dutch, German, and the Scandinavian tongues with the other Indo-European languages.

Take a more recent illustration from English alone. As late as the middle of the fourteenth century, the long vowels in English bore approximately the same relation to the characters used to represent them as they do at present in Italian, French, or German. That is, the series ā, ē, ī, open ō (approximately *aw* in *law*), close ō (approximately ō in *stone*), ū would have been pronounced about the same by an Englishman as by an Italian. By the end of the fifteenth century, these sounds had all shifted according to a regular pattern: ā became ē, open ō became close ō, close ō meanwhile had become ū, and so on. The series which had been ā, ē, ī, ō (open and close), ū was now ē, ī, ai, ō, ū, au. The final result was much the same series of sounds with which we started, but all in different places; a fact which becomes apparent to us when we first try to pronounce a foreign language. Since we have never changed our spelling to fit our pronunciation, English phonetic values are out of step with all the rest of Europe. A man of Chaucer's youth coming back a century later would probably have been able to read his native tongue, but when he heard it spoken he might well have concluded that honest English had died out, and that the people had adopted a foreign language. It is hard to see how anything could have altered more fundamentally the character of English pronunciation. The *quantity* of English vowels, if I may use my chosen terminology in a sense different from that of the linguist, was unchanged. The Great Vowel Shift neither increased nor diminished the treasury of English words. It did introduce very different notions as to what constituted "correctness" and "good taste" in the way in which English was spoken.

Three things concerning sound shifts should be remarked: First, they happen in accordance with a perfectly regular pattern. If *a*'s are shifting, *all* the *a*'s change unless some other regular linguistic tendency prevents. In the Great Vowel Shift the oral mechanism is adjusted so that each vowel is pronounced a notch higher in the mouth. (A linguist would say that the sounds were "raised.") Secondly, they happen at definite periods of history, before and after which the sounds in question show no tendency to shift. By the time Old English *stān* (which is Chaucer's *stoon,* rhyming with *lawn*) had become Modern English *stone,* the tendency for ō to become ū (as in Old English *dōm,* Modern English *doom*) had ceased, otherwise *stone* would have gone on to *stoon* (rhyming with *moon*). And thirdly, nobody knows why any of these shifts happened. Linguists have theories, but no theory has very wide acceptance, and the general run of linguists are content to accept the data, without any theory of causation at all. One thing seems pretty clear: the shifts were not due to any change in the vocal organs themselves. They resulted from an extensive reorganization of the "hookups" in the brain by which the vocal organs are directed. Men no doubt intended to do what speakers of the language had formerly been doing, but the new hookups resulted in their ordering their vocal organs to do something else.

"To accept the data, without any theory of causation at all" is not to give up the doctrine of causation, nor to say that such things as vowel shifts do not have causes. Nothing forbids us to extend the nexus of cause and effect indefinitely. Practically, however, we have to determine at what point such a method ceases to be profitable. You can say, if you wish, that these things follow an inexorable logic, but that the logic is so complex and obscure that any definitions we are likely to make now will falsify the situation by over-simplifying it. Consequently, we shall accept the vowel shifts as a starting point, without going behind them. This method has proved very fruitful in the modern science of linguistics, which could hardly have come into existence until scholars had agreed to abandon the old methods of formal grammar and the notion of fixed rules for correctness in speech; in short, to stop talking about the *why* of speech and to investigate the *how.* We do not know *why* the Great Vowel Shift occurred, but we can give a pretty full report as to the vowels actually used in a given part of England at a given time.

Linguists do not think of maintaining any more that one set of sounds is intrinsically "better" than another. For a linguist "correctness" in speech is simply the accepted usage of the time, and he expects usage to vary widely and unpredictably from one period to another. Opposed to his position is that of the purist, to whom language is static and governed by established authorities or fixed rules. Correct pronunciation for him is the first pronunciation indicated by Webster (usually an old edition of Webster); correctness in grammar is determined by a rule. "It is me" is incorrect because the construction calls for a nominative and "me" is always objective; "none of them are here" is incorrect because "none" is shown by its etymology to be singular. To the scientific linguist, such rules, if they have any validity at all, are descriptive rather than prescriptive: they describe what has occurred in the language at some time or other, but they do not have power to fix language in that pattern.

It is my notion that the dogmatic critic of literary form corresponds to the purist in language. For it seems clear to me that the basis of feeling suffers extraordinary shifts at given historical points, and that it is these shifts which mark off the "periods" in literature. The organization of our mental faculties, because of the complexity of the nervous mechanism, never achieves more than a precarious stability. Every position into which the mechanism settles contains some unbalanced tension that finally throws the system beyond the point at which the stable configuration can be recovered. A complicated process of readjustment ensues, and the system finally settles down in another precariously stable arrangement, perhaps very different from that which preceded it.

I shall now formulate succinctly as a series of theses or postulates some of the logical consequences of this theory:

1) *Poetry always expresses the basis of feeling (or sensibility) of the age in which it was written.*

2) *Critics of the past were as well qualified to apply a subjective test to poetry as we are.* ("The presumption that it is we who are more nearly at rest has no serious foundation; it is mere self-flattery.")

3) *Poetry is whatever has been called poetry by respectable judges at any time and in any place.* ("Respectable" may be thought to beg the question. I mean to include in the term those critics who had the esteem of their own age, as well as those whom we admire.)

4) *The poetry of an age never goes wrong.* Culture may go wrong, civilization may go wrong, criticism may go wrong, but poetry, in the collective sense, cannot go wrong.

II

THE DOCTRINE OF
CRITICAL RELATIVISM

I⊤ SEEMED best to me in my first lecture to sketch my entire argument with regard to the relative nature of critical judgments, leaving certain necessary but disjointed comments to be presented in this. Having disposed of these, I shall go on to discuss the function of criticism in a relativistic scheme.

Some of you will have wished to ask me whether my parallel between "classical" physics and "classical" criticism really means anything. Is it anything more than an obfuscating analogy? Relativity theory in physics resulted from a famous experiment which was not devised as a basis for relativity theory at all. In 1887 Michelson and Morley set up an apparatus for measuring the "absolute" velocity of the earth—not its velocity with regard to the sun, but the resultant of all velocities it might have with regard to the fixed and motionless ether through which it was supposed to be sweeping. As physical apparatuses go, it was not complicated: you will find in the fourteenth *Britannica* a clear description under "Michelson" and also under "Relativity" (a beautiful article by Sir James Jeans). The measure adopted was the velocity of light, which, though it moves at the tremendous speed of 186,000 miles a second, still has a finite and measurable velocity. In this apparatus light from a source was divided and sent along two arms fixed at right angles to each other; at the end of each arm was a mirror which reflected the light back to the source. Obviously on the hypothesis of the fixed ether, the time required for the beam of light to go and return should have been different in the arm which lay in the direction of the earth's motion from that in the arm which was set at right angles, and hence was turned across the line of motion. In spite of patient refinements, no difference was ever detected. The only acceptable explanation for this negative result is that the arm lying in the direction of the earth's motion contracts just enough to conceal the difference in time required for the beams to come and go—or rather, contracts just enough to make the time identical in both arms. It having been proved that an indefinable variable enters into all our measurements of lengths, spaces, and volumes, nothing remains but to accept these measurements as relative. What similar proof can be advanced that our critical measures of aesthetic value have no absolute standing? Where is the Michelson-Morley experiment of critical theory?

So long as we insist on dealing with the whole complex of the critical act, it is clear that there is none, and that it will never be possible to devise one. If it had been possible, theory of poetry would long since have been recognized as a branch of physics, and Sir Arthur Eddington would have devoted some part of *his* Messenger lectures to it. Literary theory would, at any given period, have been generally in agreement. If two theorists differed, one would have been able to invite his rival either to perform his experiments over again, with precautions to remove suspected error, or else to consider an alternative interpretation of superior scientific logic. And other theorists would not long have balanced between the two. After a little it would be found that they had practically all gone over to one theory and abandoned the other. Which is very different from what has been happening in literary theory since Plato. Aristotle's scientific works can properly be called outmoded, but his *Poetics* is, after twenty-two centuries, as good as anything that has ever been written on the subject.

But you will remember that I do not propose to apply relativity theory to the whole complex of the critical act. I propose to divide that act into two judgments, one of expressive form and the other of subject matter or moral content. The theory of the second judgment seems to me to fit very inadequately into a naturalistic scheme, and I propose to develop it by quite other assumptions. The theory of the first judgment, so far as it can be made truly psychological, *can* be handled in a naturalistic scheme, and it is so that I propose to handle it. If it is so handled, the Michelson-Morley experiment is a legitimate illustration, and theory of poetry may so far be assimilated to physical science. It is true that the nature of the materials is such that it will always be impossible to devise a simple and decisive experiment like that of Michelson and Morley. Their observed facts were scientifically controlled: that is, they were obtained by the use of a precision instrument devised for the particular purpose, an instrument operated by trained observers who made such a record of the experiment that it could be repeated in exact detail by any one who questioned their results.

The "observed facts" with which theory of poetry deals are the whole of the history of literature. The data are not controlled as a scientist would like to have them, and are not subject to such control. The experiments cannot be repeated. The observers have not recorded their results in a style even remotely satisfactory to the scientist.

Yet though the materials, even when limited to that portion pertinent to the judgment of expressive form, are not capable of being marshaled in the precise and exactly defined manner of an experiment in physics, they may still be analyzed by naturalistic principles. The difference between theories in physics and theory of poetry need not be in the kind of mental operations involved. You will remember that the results of the Michelson-Morley experiment were purely negative. The apparatus just showed nothing at all. The theory of relativity is an attempt to explain why those results were negative. The apparatus was incapable of explaining itself: no apparatus ever tells you why. And the theory of relativity was not the only possible explanation. It could have been concluded from that experiment that the Copernican cosmology, in spite of the brilliant reputation it had enjoyed for three centuries, was after all inadequate, and that we should return to the Ptolemaic, which represented the earth as the center of the universe and absolutely at rest. Of course we should have had to furbish up the Ptolemaic system with further mechanical complications to account for the astronomical observations of the last four centuries, but I have no doubt that our experts in celestial mechanics could have patched up something that would have answered, at least for the nonce. So far as I know, no one considered that explanation for a moment. The Ptolemaic cosmology was finally abandoned because it was desperately complicated and could be made to account for the increasing wealth of data obtained by observation only by making it more complicated, whereas Copernicus's cosmology would do everything the Ptolemaic did and do it more simply. In fact, Copernicus's system itself proved capable of further simplification. The scientific mind rebels against a tangled machine of spheres and epicycles to explain the motion of the outer planets around the earth, when the whole thing can be so much more simply explained by assuming that the earth, like Jupiter and Saturn, is a satellite of the sun, and that the planets move in elliptical orbits. That is why I said the theory of relativity is not the only, but the only acceptable, explanation of the negative results of the Michelson-Morley experiment. *It is the simplest explanation which will cover the observed facts.*

Now we have to interpret literary history just as scientists had to interpret the Michelson-Morley experiment. And although the evidence is so ambiguous that we are not likely to attain to unanimity of opinion, we can still frame our theories in the naturalistic manner. That means, in brief, that in order to be respectable, an explanation must cover the facts, and that of two alternative explanations that cover the facts, the simpler is to be preferred.

The fact of revolutions in taste will not be disputed. The critical judgments of one age are always repudiated by the age that comes after. The Restoration sneers at the

Elizabethan critics, the Romantics sneer at the eighteenth century, we sneer at the Victorians. Each age, with a fine feeling of superiority, writes its critical predecessors off either as stupid or unfortunate—unfortunate in not having the perspective or skill of the moderns.

This is no doubt the commonest of the assumptions underlying absolutist judgments in criticism: the assumption of a progression of taste, of an accumulation of critical knowledge which makes the later age always clearer-sighted. I should say that it ought to be dismissed because it does not cover the facts, and cannot be made to cover them. If one really invoked it consistently, he would have to believe that critical doctrine, by and large, has been getting better from the Elizabethan age (to go no further back) to the present. Of course what is true by and large is not necessarily true of particular critics, but we should at least *expect* to find Dryden a sounder critic than Ben Jonson, Samuel Johnson sounder than Dryden, Coleridge sounder than Samuel Johnson, Arnold sounder than Coleridge, Paul Elmer More and T. S. Eliot soundest of all. In science that would be just what one would find, for science *is* progressive. Though one would hesitate to say that anybody ever was or ever would be a greater scientific genius than Sir Isaac Newton, we should expect the scientific theories of Faraday and Maxwell to be "sounder" than Newton's, and those of Planck, Einstein, and Bohr to be "sounder" still. Science cumulates, criticism does nothing of the sort. Indeed there is a rather marked tendency in criticism to repudiate the judgments of the ages nearest our own, and to revive those of an earlier period.

There seems to be no reason at all for concluding that

taste grows progressively better, or that the mere passage of time widens literary sympathies and sharpens the critical faculty. The eighteenth century lost Donne, who for our modern poets and critics is almost the touchstone. Our age has regained Donne but has lost Pope. It looks as though the next generation might regain Pope at the expense of losing Shelley. I recommend the rejection of the explanation of progression in taste, then, as not really explaining history at all.

Another, and better, theory admits the relative nature of untutored or illiterate judgments, but holds out, at least as an ideal, the possibility of absolute judgments in those who have equipped themselves with the necessary education. This, if I understand him, is Croce's position. It is true, he would say, that a boy or an adult of limited education would find the poetry of many periods of the past unintelligible, or, if intelligible, dull. That is only to be expected. Every poem was the expression of a particular mind, located at a particular point in history. If we are to see what the poet saw, we must place ourselves where he stood. We can do that by research: by giving our minds the same content as his. I like this theory because it is sober and learned; because it challenges the facile journalism that passes so frequently for criticism. It would seem to me obvious that one cannot fully understand Shakespeare or Milton or Pope without becoming a good deal of an antiquary. And I do not share the contempt of some of our bright young men for annotation. I am myself a devoted and insatiable writer of footnotes. But when I am honest with myself, I have to admit that erudition, though it gives understanding (a very precious thing), never by itself confers the rapture of intuitive poetic experience. Just as, by study of relativity theory, I can come to understand that people on a planet moving at a different velocity from mine would call a rectangle a square, so I can come to understand that to an organization of sensibility different from my own the rules were a valid definition of dramatic form, and satire the satisfaction of the nobler instincts of poetry. I can even bring myself to admit that my squares would be rectangles to people of that sensibility, and that they have as good a right to their opinion as I have to mine. But perfect understanding and charity will never make their rectangles *look square* to me. Erudition must finally be applied through a sensibility, and our sensibility seems to me as stubborn as the accent of our speech. I must myself reject this explanation, because I cannot convince myself that it covers the facts, but I greatly prefer it to any which maintains a progression in taste.

A third theory is that formulated by Wordsworth, and held consciously or unconsciously by many critics. According to this view, the taste of all periods is generally bad. All writing that history records is "stained with the peculiarities" of its age. But there is a correct, "permanent" style which can be not only defined but also exemplified. I have made Wordsworth's criticism the subject of special attention in my next lecture, but I must pause here to anticipate some of my objections to his position.

One may well question, if the taste of all past ages proves upon examination to be so bad, how can one be sure that his own is not worse? Where is the ποῦ στῆναι? How does one derive his notion of this permanently correct way of writing? But I should reject this explanation on another ground: its lack of simplicity. It is like the machinery of the epicycles. For what recourse could be more desperate than that of accusing all the great authors of the past of bad taste? Is it not simpler and a great deal more satisfactory to abandon as meaningless the search for an absolutely good style, and to agree that good taste in literature is, like good taste in language, the expression of sensibility in accordance with the accepted usage of the time? To agree that our original critical judgments are, in the final analysis, subjective; and that the sensibility or basis of feeling to which we refer for a measurement is a variable whose characteristics can be recorded historically after they are past, but whose future changes are unpredictable?

What likelihood is there that we are better equipped to criticize Pope than Dr. Johnson was? We know a great deal about Johnson. In spite of certain prejudices, he seems on the whole to have been one of the ablest of English critics. Why should he go wrong when he maintained that if Pope was not a poet he knew not where poetry was to be found? If it can be argued that he was incapacitated by being of Pope's own age, it can be argued with much greater plausibility that he was by that very fact better equipped to enter into Pope's poetry and report on what is to be found there. We assume too easily that "perspective" is to be preferred to proximity.

We make a mistake when we assume (as we all do) that poets throughout the ages have been working at the same problem. That is a false analogy from science. Aristotle and David Starr Jordan would have been working on the same problem if each had attempted a biological description of a species of fish; if they failed to agree, it would be quite correct to say that one of them was wrong. But Homer and Milton were not working at the same problem. In poetry each age has a *unique* problem, and it is the part of wisdom as well as of charity to suppose that each age solved its problem about as well as it could be solved.

Hence my theses that critics of the past were as well qualified as we to apply a subjective test to poetry, and that consequently poetry is whatever has been called poetry by respectable judges at any time and in any place. If Percival Stockdale says that Pope moved him to raptures, I shall not call him a liar, or assume that he had desperately bad taste. I shall accept his report as true, and regret that I cannot get from Pope what he got. My consolation is that I can get a considerable amount of excitement from Donne, and that he probably could not. Much less shall I argue with Scott and Byron when one tells me that Johnson's *Vanity of Human Wishes* extracts tears from the eyes and the other says that in passion Pope surpasses the Romantics.

Poetry in the bulk, poetry by and large, infallibly expresses the sensibility of the age which produced it. If it did not, it would not be poetry at all. And hence I say that poetry, in the collective sense, cannot go wrong. Any given author may have written a partially bad poem, or a wholly bad poem, or a whole series of bad poems. But, like Burke, I do not know the method of drawing up an indictment against a whole people. We must look with extreme suspicion on statements to the effect that in the reign of James I or Charles II poetry wandered off the right track, and did not find it again until *Lyrical Ballads* or *The Waste*

Land. Poetry has never got off the track. It cannot get off the track. It has, at all times and in all places, been faithfully occupied with the only materials on which poetry can work, those that express the sensibility of the age.

That is not to say that civilization cannot go wrong. I am not a moral relativist, though I cannot convict of logical error any man who chooses to be one. It will be enough if I insist that relativism in physics and in theory of poetry does not imply as a logical consequence relativism in matters of faith and morals. That is something to be settled by experience, not by *a priori* argument. Is it strange that experience should indicate that some things in the structure of being are best regarded as fixed and others as not? I subscribe without reservation to a Christian orthodoxy and its attendant moral code, because from participating in the Church's life I have come to believe that its dogmatic pronouncements are *true;* not true because man constructed them himself, in the sense that Newton's laws of motion were constructed, but because, to use theological language, they were supernaturally revealed. Religion is for me the fixed center about which other things move. But I cannot persuade myself that God has seen fit to reveal a critical orthodoxy, or to announce an absolute standard of taste. Theory of poetry, as I am presenting it, is naturalistic; and, like natural science and natural religion, it does not aspire above relativism.

If you wish to argue that the social organization of the eighteenth century caused greater misery among the laboring classes than that of the nineteenth, that seems to me a legitimate topic for a debate. If you believe that the clergy of the eighteenth century were less sensitive

33

in the performance of the vows of their sacred calling than their predecessors of the seventeenth, I shall grant you the right to present your evidence. I should not regard as nonsense the proposition that the political morality of Sir Robert Walpole was less admirable than that of Mr. Winston Churchill, or that our prisons are more humane than those of the days of Fielding. In short, if you wish to contend that civilization generally, or any part of it, went wrong in the neo-classic period or in the Romantic, you will find me an interested listener.

But the attack should be against the civilization, not against the poetry. When a river changes its course, we may regret it and feel that the old course was more beautiful or more convenient. But if we want to float our boats, we must go where the water is. How often have critics been urging poets to tug their boats over the shingle of the dry river bed! If a poet in any age tries artificially to express what he does not feel, the result will not be poetry. We should not ask for poetry breathing the pure religion of Nature from an urbane skeptical century, nor poetry of clarity and serenity from a perplexed and despondent people. What we can ask of the poetry of an age is that it shall express the sensibility of that age. And that is what poetry in the gross always and inevitably does without our asking.

What, then, becomes of our quantitative judgments? What grounds have we for saying that Shakespeare was "greater" than Dryden, or Wordsworth "greater" than Shelley? On the whole, I think it would be a good thing for the study of literature if we were a little less anxious about assigning the exact degrees of greatness. Why spoil our pleasure in the poems of William Morris by badgering ourselves with scruples as to whether or not Tennyson is greater? The evidence for many of the traditional verdicts of "great" is pretty disreputable, especially that which concerns authors who lived before the invention of printing. Sheer accident has played an uncomfortably large part in determining what works have come down to us. Gothic poetry is entirely lost. Nearly all the Old English poetry we know is preserved in four codices, which give duplicate texts for only one poem, and that a short one. Is it likely that these chance-recovered waifs preserve the best of a rich and varied literature? We have lost the greater part of Livy, but we have a full text of the *Punica* of Silius Italicus. An impartial judgment might conclude that some of the Elizabethan plays studied in college classes are really inferior to many ephemeral Broadway successes. We pay attention to them because relatively few plays from that period have survived.

Yet these skeptical remarks would be meaningless apart from the assumption that some authors *are* "greater" than others. Dogmatic critics explain greatness by saying that certain authors have approximated more closely than others to the enduring principles of true art. I should prefer to say that the "great" authors have produced works which, for a variety of reasons, contain greater value than others, without assuming that the values found in them by different individuals or different ages have been just the same. Enduring greatness in literature means richness or complexity of value on many levels. Scott, says Governor Cross in a paragraph capable of wider application, "hit upon a kind of novel elastic enough to contain about everything in fiction which pleases; and he thereby appealed to various orders of mind. For the romantic he had his gorgeous scenes; for lovers of mystery he had secrets to be disclosed in the third volume, and sliding panels and trap doors for the entrances and exits of ghosts; for lovers of wild adventure he had caves, prisons, crypts, bandits, and hairbreadth escapes; for those who turn to the novel for a description of manners he furnished probably as accurate transcripts of real life as are to be found in the professed realists." The same could be said, *mutatis mutandis*, for Homer or Vergil or Dante or Shakespeare. Shakespeare has been praised from Dryden's time to ours, but if you will examine Shakespearean criticism chronologically, you will find that he is being praised for different things at different times, and that in detail the different appraisals pretty much cancel one another. History, in other words, appears to indicate that Shakespeare is sufficiently complex to maintain the respect of readers through all possible shifts of sensibility; and that Pope is not, though during his periods of popularity he may be more intensely admired. In this sense, if one thinks it worth while, he can classify Pope as an author of the second rank, but the historical grounds for doing so are very different from the dogmatic.

I was led into these considerations by a study of Wordsworth's strictures on the poetry of the eighteenth century. And the eighteenth century does need a lot of explaining. Its poetry suffered greater eclipse than that of other periods because the reorganization of sensibility which marked the beginning of the Romantic period was more extensive and violent than usual. It is abundantly clear that in eighteenth-century sensibility feelings were tied to the general; men were excited by generalizations, not by particulars. Men then felt the imagined norm to be more real, more exciting, more poetical, than any particular example. The most famous statement of the principle occurs in the tenth chapter of *Rasselas*, but Sir Joshua Reynolds furnishes several formulations which are even more telling:

"Thus amongst the blades of grass or leaves of the same tree, though no two can be found exactly alike, the general form is invariable; a Naturalist, before he chose one as a sample, would examine many; since if he took the first that occurred, it might have, by accident or otherwise, such a form as that it would scarce be known to belong to that species; he selects as the painter does, the most beautiful, that is, the most general form of nature. . . .

"The terms beauty, or nature, which are general ideas, are but different modes of expressing the same thing, whether we apply these terms to statues, poetry, or pictures. Deformity is not nature, but an accidental deviation from her accustomed practice. This general idea, therefore, ought to be called Nature; and nothing else, correctly speaking, has a right to that name. . . . It plainly appears, that as a work is conducted under the influence of general ideas, or partial, it is principally to be considered as the effect of a good or a bad taste. . . .

"This great ideal perfection and beauty are not to be sought in the heavens, but upon the earth. They are about us, and upon every side of us. But the power of discovering what is deformed in nature, or, in other words, what is particular and uncommon, can be acquired only by experience; and the whole beauty and grandeur of the art consists, in my opinion, in being able to get above all singular forms, local custom, particularities, and details of every kind."

Men of the eighteenth century did not say things like that because they were depraved or because they had false taste. They said them simply and solely because particularizations seemed to them prosaic, while generalizations made their beards bristle and sent tremors up and down their spines. And, through historical accident, culture was less varied in that age than in any other of modern times. The poetry of the eighteenth century is much more of a piece than that of the seventeenth or the nineteenth. Consequently, when sensibility shifted violently, and men turned to the individual concrete object as the real thing and repudiated generalizations as unreal, the whole expanse of eighteenth-century poetry became more or less inaccessible.

It seems now to be generally assumed without question that the particular *is* the poetical, and that the general is, by definition, anti-poetical. This is only an illegitimate erection of the Romantic temperament into a dogma. So far as I can see, it all depends on the way in which your sensibility is organized, which is a matter for historical investigation, not for *a priori* theorizing. The eighteenth century furnishes impressive testimony to the fact that in those days human beings thrilled naturally to lines in which fish are less often fish than they are the finny tribe or the scaly breed. If it happened once, it can happen again. To assume that *our* sensibility is right is only self-flattery.

And the same may be said of our preferences among

the various genres. Since the advent of Romanticism, it seems to have been generally agreed that satire is hardly a form of poetry. From any historical point of view this is heresy pure and simple. The total bulk of satire (even of formal satire) in ancient and modern literatures is enormous. The depreciation of satire is only another aspect of the attempt to set up the Romantic sensibility as the absolute definition. Art is long: many sensibilities will come after ours.

A word, too, about the "rules," so offensive to us, and certainly false if presented as final and exclusive. Did not poetry which followed the rules go astray?

> But ye were dead
> To things ye knew not of,—were closely wed
> To musty laws lined out with wretched rule
> And compass vile: so that ye taught a school
> Of dolts to smooth, inlay, and clip, and fit,
> Till, like the certain wands of Jacob's wit,
> Their verses tallied.

Was Keats totally wrong? Not *poetically* wrong at all, for he is defining by negation his own idea of poetry. *Critically* very young, I should say, very angry, and very wrong. Poetry never followed rules unwillingly. We should not think of the rules as manacles clamped on the struggling limbs of poets by a police force of rationalists. They were rather the spontaneous *definition* of the neo-classic temperament, and in their formulation the poets themselves eagerly collaborated. As soon as the rules really became manacles, that is as soon as they really ceased to be expressive for genuine poets, they were discarded.

I hope it will not be inferred from this that I see no value

39

in the historical study of absolutist theories of poetry. Nearly all studies in theory of poetry are valuable in defining the sensibility of the age that produced them: something that to the historical critic is as important as the definition of his own. But he must ignore their assumptions that the real right kind of poetry is now being given its final definition.

Of course I do not mean that critics should give up the whole game in despair and attempt no evaluation at all. Our physicists did not stop measuring when they lost their confidence in the absolute nature of their measures. The measures were just as useful as they ever were. Relativity doctrine, as a matter of fact, does not affect the practical business of measuring. It is a philosophy concerning the nature of measuring as such.

Critics should evaluate, and evaluate with all their might. But they ought to realize that what they are really evaluating is their own sensibility—or, if that sounds too much like a paradox, that they are always evaluating in terms of their own sensibility. The question, what is the poetry of Shakespeare, if taken in any absolute sense, may as well be dismissed. But the question, what has the poetry of Shakespeare seemed like to representative human beings, including myself, is a proper question. We cannot put Pope in his place for all time, but we can put ourselves on record for all time with regard to Pope. If we experience profound physiological disturbances when we read Blake and not when we read Pope, that is something to write down. It is not merely our privilege, it is our duty to write it down. But we should not go on to say that Pope is not a poet and that Blake is. We should say that by the imperious testimony of our own sensibilities Blake is a poet of remarkable power. Pope, on the other hand, is a poet whom a shift in basis of feeling has rendered largely inaccessible to us. How do we know that he is a poet? Because a long succession of respectable critics and poets—Gray, Johnson, Byron—tell us so. What better authority could we ask for?

And there, I think, is a fair epitome of literary criticism as it should be written. It should begin with an honest and unflinching statement of the critic's own successes in reading. He will approach every poem of the past patiently, sympathetically, and hopefully, but he will not pretend to raptures that he does not feel. He will describe carefully and honestly just what comes through to him and no more. That is one half of criticism, the subjective or personal. But he will recognize his judgment for what it is: the report of a sensitive mechanism significantly different from that of his predecessors. Though he will make use of all the erudition he can muster, he will not pretend that he has been able to put himself back at the exact point where the poet stood when he "saw" the poem. First, foremost, and all the time he will be *humble:* he will assume, until evidence to the contrary appears, that his predecessors had mechanisms as sensitive as his own and were as honest in reporting what their mechanisms brought through to *them.* He will be pleased when his judgment coincides with theirs, but he will be even more pleased when he finds himself better equipped to exploit some particular area of poetry than they were. Frequently he will have to confess a limitation: "There is undoubtedly poetic value of a high order here, but I am insensitive to it." In other words, the true critic will know that poetry—or, let us say, a poem—is an immortal thing. His criticism is only a bit of its ever-expanding life. The whole poem is his criticism plus all the other criticism it has evoked. To his own evaluation the critic will add a selection from what critics of the past have said about it, by no means limiting himself to judgments that coincide with his own. That is the other half of criticism, the historical.

The subjective judgment plus the historical record. But what shall be the procedure of the critic who is dealing with contemporary literature? That must be the subject of our next lecture.

III

THE CRITIC'S

RESPONSIBILITY

In my discussion of shifts in the basis of feeling, I probably gave the impression that these shifts took place over night in the entire population. This is of course not true. The shift took place separately, it may be at widely different times, in all the individuals making up the population. Let us return to our useful analogy of linguistic shifts. We have unmistakable evidence that the Great Vowel Shift had begun to operate in the speech of some individuals a hundred years before the new vowel pattern had become standard—that is, had become the pronunciation accepted by the majority as preferable. If you had taken a cross-section of English speech at any time during that century, you would have found one group of speakers in whom the shift had made little progress. Their way of speaking would have been considered old-fashioned. In another group, the shift would have gone pretty far, so far that their pronunciation would have been called affected. In between would be the bulk of the population, employing a pronunciation in which the individual differences would not be striking enough to attract attention,

43

and who would probably have been unaware of the fact that their pronunciation was changing. Actually, no two persons in the entire population would have shown exactly the same vowels. But a linguist could have grouped them with reference to the Vowel Shift, and could have seen in which direction the shift was tending. The same thing appears in shifts of sensibility. It was but two years after the death of Pope that Joseph Warton wrote the preface to his little volume of odes; and his *Essay on the Writings and Genius of Pope* followed only ten years later. In both he reveals—and what is more, defines clearly and memorably—the full-blown Romantic sensibility half a century before the publication of *Lyrical Ballads*. On the other hand William Gifford shows the typical neo-classical sensibility in the heyday of the Romantics. He was born in the year of the publication of Warton's *Essay*, and he outlived Byron, Shelley, and Keats.

The process may be likened to an avalanche. Hurtling boulders and detached masses of snow indicate the precarious stability of the whole heap; the projectile fragments come more closely together, and then with a tremendous roar the body of the avalanche comes down all at once, though laggard masses follow one by one, some of them days later. The great shift from neo-classic to Romantic must have begun while Pope was at the very height of his powers. By the time of the publication of *Lyrical Ballads* it had not gone very far, as the abuse heaped upon that volume indicates. Scott and Byron, more than any other literary forces, loosened the snow, and the avalanche came down, one would guess, not much before 1830. In blaming Wordsworth for his "later" manner we choose to for-

get that he was born in 1770 and that Samuel Rogers
outlived him. The "later" manner was really an earlier manner which he did not display at the time one would have
expected it. The miracle is that any man born fourteen
years before the death of Dr. Johnson should have been
able to write the type pieces of the Romantic revolt.

It does not follow that because Joseph Warton shows
the full-blown Romantic sensibility in 1746 he was therefore able to write full-blown Romantic poetry. Poets who
precede the avalanche too far are doomed to be, if not
mute inglorious Miltons, at least thwarted and inexpres-
sive Miltons. Mr. T. S. Eliot has done great service in
giving us the concept and terminology of "poetic idiom."
Each sensibility has an idiom which is perfectly expressive
of it. But the two are two things: the sensibility may develop before the idiom is enounced, or the idiom may go
on being used conventionally after the sensibility has
changed. At the beginning of a shift in sensibility, and perhaps long after the beginning, poets continue to use the
old idiom because they know no other. Awkwardly and by
half-lights the new sensibility shows through, striving for
more perfect expression. Then the idiom is enounced: let
us say, Kyd's dramatic blank verse, Waller's couplets, Coleridge's *Ancient Mariner* and *Christabel,* Eliot's *Waste Land,*
or perhaps the poetry of Ezra Pound. Before this time a
great poetic genius might fumble at expression, after it the
rankest poetaster can write with ease in the new style. All
the world can now speak the idiom: all the world can
have the flower, for all have got the seed.

A pertinent example is Sir Walter Scott's poetry. He
had to hear snatches of William Taylor's unpublished

45

translation of *Lenore* before he could write his early pieces; and he had to hear a recitation of *Christabel* before he could bring *The Lay of the Last Minstrel* to birth. Notice in both cases that the model which worked such impressive results was an unpublished poem which Scott had no opportunity to study in detail. Yet the effect was instantaneous—like the freezing of super-cooled water when an ice crystal is dropped into it. Though an unoriginal poet so far as "idiom" is concerned, he became one of the most facile and influential verse-writers of his time.

The chief function of the critic of contemporary literature is to recognize and to define the emergent idiom: to detach it from the background of the moribund but highly respectable idiom which obscures it. He should realize that he has little or no power to change its essential character or direction; no more, let us say, than the linguist has to change the development of language. Nothing is more futile than to scold an O'Neill because he has not written like Aeschylus, or an Eliot for not having written like Tennyson. Jeffrey's criticism of Wordsworth is a classical example of the folly of the judicial method. So far as he defined the real character of the Wordsworthian sensibility, even when he did it with malice, he performed a useful function. But in that part of his criticism on which he seems chiefly to have prided himself—his magisterial directions to Wordsworth to mend his ways by the imitation of better models—he did no good to his public or to Wordsworth, and he hurt his own reputation. His task, like that of every other critic of contemporary authors, was to help to disengage the new idiom from the old, to facilitate its emergence. He should not have insisted that the new idiom be pleasant to him. If a critic is past thirty-five, it is fairly certain that his taste is pretty well hardened, and that no really new style will delight him much. But he can console himself with two reflections: history always justifies every way of writing once it has established itself, and the new way will come whether he opposes it or not.

None of the great English critics can be held in all respects to exemplify the method I am recommending. But I think that if Dryden had followed up the promise of his earliest critical writing, we might have had a model. It is true that he had his limitations, serious ones. His religious progress seems to me sincere; if his writings after 1685 do not breathe genuine and affecting piety, I do not know how to recognize the signs. And the flattery in his works which is to us so offensive—all that fulsome praise of the characters and writings of Dorset and Normanby—we should try to make some allowance for, for it was a convention of the times. No man, as Dr. Johnson said, is upon oath in epitaphs or dedications, and a discouraging amount of Dryden's critical writings consists of dedications. Yet in spite of all that can be said, Dryden's moral character was something too facile and accommodating. We cannot rid ourselves of the suspicion that *he* would have dedicated the *Dictionary* to Chesterfield after all.

Three times every year it is my unhappy lot to examine doctoral candidates in their knowledge of English literature, and three times each year I hear Dryden treated with easy contempt by our young people because he changed his mind and reversed his judgments so often. I should have supposed that that was his great glory. You can find in

Dryden, if you ignore his argument and cling to his *obiter dicta*, an extended, patient, and extremely acute effort to define the emerging sensibility of his age: to state the idiom, not as possessing absolute validity, but as proper for his own time.

You must ignore his argument, though. I have been reading in Dryden's criticism for the last twenty years, and always go back to it with pleasant anticipation. After writing that last sentence I paused and read the two volumes of Ker's collection straight through—and with growing dismay. Like Dr. Johnson on hearing *Irene*, I thought it had been better. The greater part of the expanse of the essays is a desert, not bare, for it supports a very handsome collection of desert plants—the graceful blooms of Dryden's style. But it is hack work, and not the hack work of a man like Johnson, whose mind always grapples with his subject matter; it is wholesale pillaging of Le Bossu and Rapin and Boileau and Rymer by a clever man of letters whose mind is hardly on his job. One does not know whether to laugh or cry when he finds things like this:

> "Homer and Virgil are to be our guides in the Epic; Sophocles and Euripides in Tragedy: in all things we are to imitate the customs and the times of those persons and things which we represent: not to make new rules of the drama, as Lopez de Vega has attempted unsuccessfully to do, but to be content to follow our masters, who understood Nature better than we."

But when Dryden, in defiance of consistency, follows the bent of his "natural diffidence and scepticism," how inimitable he is! There is nothing so *right* as the following in all the criticism of Johnson or Arnold:

"It is to raise envy to the living to compare them with the dead. They are honoured and almost adored by us, as they deserve; neither do I know any so presumptuous of themselves as to contend with them. Yet give me leave to say thus much without injury to their ashes: that not only we shall never equal them, but they could never equal themselves were they to rise and write again. We acknowledge them our fathers in wit; but they have ruined their estates themselves, before they came to their children's hands. There is scarce an humour, a character, or any kind of plot, which they have not blown upon. All comes sullied or wasted to us; and were they to entertain this age, they could not make so plenteous treatments out of such decayed fortunes. This therefore will be a good argument to us either not to write at all, or to attempt some other way. There is no bays to be expected in their walks: *tentanda via est, qua me quoque possum tollere humo.*

"This way of writing in verse they have only left free to us; our age is arrived to a perfection in it which they never knew; and which (if we may guess by what of theirs we have seen in verse, as *The Faithful Shepherdess* and *Sad Shepherd*) 'tis probable they never could have reached. For the genius of every age is different."

This is perhaps too deprecatory, though it is wonderfully persuasive. Dryden does not attack the Elizabethans who are held up to him as models; he only insists on the necessity which each age is under to innovate on its predecessor. *Si sic ubique!*

From Dryden, then, if one does not insist on making

him appear consistent, can be gathered an impressive body of the sort of criticism which I should recommend. From him let us turn to another critic—also a poet—who has the distinction of never once deviating into relativism. It is an ungracious task to disparage Wordsworth, especially at this university. It seems merely perverse to disparage him after having said kind things about Dryden. Wordsworth appears to have had a richer poetic endowment than Dryden, as he certainly had a more profound moral sense. He was a person of the most admirable integrity, integrity coupled with a somewhat less admirable stubbornness and self-sufficiency. It is really because of his consistency that he is so useful for my purpose. Prepared as one may be for tenacity of opinion in Wordsworth, one will nevertheless be astonished to see how he managed in a body of critical writing of such bulk to avoid all relative judgments. I choose him because he is the prime example in English of a first-rate doctrinaire critic, and because his writings contain the most powerful statement that I have anywhere encountered of the view opposed to that which I am advocating. My attack is limited, of course, to Wordsworth the critic, Wordsworth the writer of prefaces. His achievement in enouncing and establishing a novel idiom is tremendous. I am at issue here only with the prose arguments by which he attempts to give this idiom general validity.

For Wordsworth has no doubt at all that it is possible to define and exemplify a way of writing poetry—an "idiom"—that is absolutely correct. If, he says in the Preface of 1800, the views with which the *Lyrical Ballads* were composed could be realized, the result would be "a class of Poetry . . . well adapted to interest mankind *permanently*." He has "a deep impression of certain inherent and indestructible qualities of the human mind, and likewise of certain powers in the great and *permanent* objects that act upon it, which are equally inherent and indestructible," and he believes that the time is approaching when the present vicious styles of poetry "will be systematically opposed." This central or ideal poetry must possess "the primary virtues of sincerity, earnestness, and a moral interest in the main object." In it "an enlightened Critic chiefly looks for a reflection of the wisdom of the heart and the grandeur of the imagination. Wherever these appear, simplicity accompanies them: Magnificence herself, when legitimate, depending upon a simplicity of her own to regulate her ornaments." That, I fear, means nothing very precise. It is a relief to turn from it to the clear, though highly controversial, statement that the ideal poetry must be written "in a selection of language really used by men." This language is essentially no different from the language of prose.

As a fact of literary history, however, this ideal or normal style of poetry hardly exists. Every age has exhibited a vicious style, a poetic diction. This has come about in the simplest possible manner. The earliest poets "wrote from passion excited by real events." In later times men ambitious of the fame of poets "set themselves to a mechanical adoption of these figures of speech" used by the poets their predecessors, often applying this language "to feelings and thoughts with which they had no natural connection whatsoever. A language was thus insensibly produced, differing materially from the real language of men in *any situation*."

Hence many modern writers are addicted to "gaudiness and inane phraseology." This is no new state of affairs; poetic style has long been in a bad way. Shakespeare himself "stooped to accommodate himself to the People." In the time of James I literature was "stuffed with quaint or out-of-the-way thoughts"; in that of Charles I "the general taste was capricious, fantastical, or grovelling"; in the time of Charles II "vicious writings . . . accorded with the public taste"; in that of Queen Anne and the first two Georges, writers in general were "seduced by the example of Pope, whose sparkling and tuneful manner had bewitched the men of letters his contemporaries, and corrupted the judgment of the nation through all ranks of society." Pope's attempts at poetry of the nobler sort are "little better than a tissue of false thoughts, languid and vague expressions, unmeaning antithesis, and laborious attempts at discrimination." An addiction to an antithetical manner of writing, in fact, is proof "that the nobler sympathies are not alive" in a man. It is the poetry of the whole age, not merely Pope's, that is thus stigmatized. "Excepting the *Nocturnal Reverie* of Lady Winchilsea and a passage or two in the *Windsor Forest* of Pope, the poetry of the period intervening between the publication of the *Paradise Lost* and the *Seasons* does not contain a single new image of external nature"; indeed, "a blind man, in the habit of attending accurately to descriptions casually dropped from the lips of those around him, might easily depict these appearances with more truth." Even Thomson (whom Wordsworth grouped with Collins and Dyer as having more poetic imagination than the other writers of the century) wrote a vicious style, his "false ornaments" being "exactly of that kind which would be most likely to strike the undiscerning." The language of the eighteenth century was generally "vague, glossy, and unfeeling." In short, to sum it all up: "The favourite style of different ages is so different and wanders so far from propriety that if it were not that first-rate Writers in all nations and tongues are governed by common principles, we might suppose that truth and nature were things not to be looked for in books." To an unpracticed reader the poetry of every age will present the obstacle of a deformity of style. Hence the magnitude of the revolution which Wordsworth set out to accomplish. It was nothing less than to make poetry and men's feelings "more sane, pure, and *permanent*, in short, more consonant to nature, that is, to eternal nature, and the great moving spirit of things."

Now there is only one question to put to a man who presents such views: How do you know that they are true? The difference between your chosen way of writing and Pope's is obvious, but what authorizes you to take yours as the standard, and to condemn Pope for vicious taste? The earth and the nebula are getting farther apart, we all agree on that, but how can you be sure that the observed velocity belongs exclusively to the nebula?

Wordsworth has given us an answer, though briefly and incidentally: it is exactly the same as Housman's. "First-rate writers in all nations and tongues are governed by common principles." And he has singled out the four "greatest" English poets: Chaucer, Shakespeare, Spenser, Milton. I should not like to have to formulate the common principles of style underlying the work of Chaucer and Milton. Chaucer and Spenser look like a more easily reducible pair, but I think they would actually prove just as refractory. Add a few more names: Homer, Sophocles, Vergil, Dante, Goethe—is it not clear that any common principles of style which you can discover for such a group will be so excessively general and vague as hardly to be worth listing? That we do not consider these men first-rate authors because they wrote on common principles but because they wrote supremely well on *different* principles?

Please do not take me to have said more than I have said. I do not think the search for a common denominator of *style* rewarding; I am an aesthetic relativist. But I am not a moral relativist. Even if one does not assign to Christian morality the absolute validity that I do, he must still grant it historical continuity. We *do* have an unchanging measure for the moral content of poetry. It *is* possible to formulate common principles by which the *subject matter* of Chaucer, Shakespeare, Spenser, and Milton can be judged. This is why dogmatic criticism tends so often to be moralistic. But Wordsworth, though there is some confusion in his argument, was talking in the main about *style*. He really believed that there was an ideal idiom, a permanently correct poetic style.

We have other material for testing the validity of Wordsworth's absolute judgments. There is that sonnet of Gray's which he condemns so confidently in the Preface of 1800. Of the fourteen lines he will allow only five to have any value.[1] Now my taste is sufficiently like his so that I agree

---

[1] "In vain to me the smiling mornings shine,
And redd'ning Phoebus lifts his golden fire:
The birds in vain their amorous descant join;
Or cheerful fields resume their green attire:

with him in finding little pleasure in reddening Phoebus
or the amorous descant of birds that complain to warm
their little loves—whatever that may mean. But what is
the matter with

> Or cheerful fields resume their green attire?

Wordsworth in 1800 rejects it because of the mild personification implied in "cheerful fields" and for the word
"attire," which then seemed to him poetic diction, but
it would be possible to parallel it with hundreds of lines
from his own "later" poetry—some of them written only
a very few years later than that preface.

Consider too that passage from Dryden's *Indian Em-
peror* which he condemns as "vague, bombastic, and sense-
less." [2] His choice of the lines was not accidental, for

> These ears, alas! for other notes repine,
>   *A different object do these eyes require.*
> *My lonely anguish melts no heart but mine;*
>   *And in my breast the imperfect joys expire.*
> Yet morning smiles the busy race to cheer,
>   And new-born pleasure brings to happier men:
> The fields to all their wonted tribute bear:
>   To warm their little loves the birds complain:
> *I fruitless mourn to him that cannot hear,*
>   *And weep the more because I weep in vain.*

"It will easily be perceived that the only part of this Sonnet which
is of any value is the lines printed in Italics."

---

[2] *Enter* CORTEZ *alone in a Night-gown.*
> All things are hush'd, as Nature's self lay dead;
> The Mountains seem to nod their drowsie Head;
> The little Birds in Dreams their Songs repeat,
> And sleeping Flowers beneath the Night-dew sweat:
> Ev'n Lust and Envy sleep; yet Love denies
> Rest to my Soul, and Slumber to my Eyes.
>   *The Indian Emperor*, III. ii. 1–6.

Rymer, by singling them out for extravagant praise, had made them a touchstone for neo-classical taste, and Wordsworth wishes to make his heresy emphatic and shocking. We shall, I think, feel like agreeing with him. But what right have we to say that our taste is better than Rymer's? It is too easy to say that Rymer, in his other judgments, shows that his taste is bad. *How do you know?* Where is your fixed point of reference? Will you dispose of Dr. Johnson in the same way? In his notes to *Macbeth* he has balanced that passage against one of the most admired in Shakespeare and declines to give Shakespeare's the palm. It is also possible to bring Johnson and Wordsworth into direct collision in their judgments on Pope's epitaph on Mrs. Corbet. Johnson praises it, saying that it contains "scarce one line taken from commonplaces." Wordsworth, admitting merit in two and a half lines out of ten, condemns the epitaph as a whole for being "cold and unfeeling"; says that the thoughts "are entangled in vicious expression"; and that the "point" of the last line is a "playing with the Reader's fancy, to the delusion and dishonour of his understanding."

Yet in the analysis of this epitaph Wordsworth says one very illuminating thing. Epitaphs, he remarks, *should* "contain thoughts and feelings which are in their substance commonplace, and even trite." But these commonplaces "should be uttered in such connection as shall make it felt that they are not adopted, not spoken by rote, but perceived in their whole compass *with the freshness and clearness of an original intuition.*"

Of course. No better description of poetry was ever written. All true poetry perceives its object in its whole compass and utters it with the freshness and clearness of an original intuition. But what if this idiom, so hackneyed and devitalized in 1810, was supple and youthful in 1730? What if the structure of Pope's sensibility was such that his original intuitions clothed themselves in point and antithesis? What if, in that age, "reasoning in verse" carried the unreasonable excitement of poetry? What if, in Mrs. Corbet's day, tenderness and pathos could be packed into an epigram? That, surely, is a simpler and more credible hypothesis than the one which accuses a whole age—and all ages—of vicious taste.

IV

WHAT IS POETRY?

A DISTINGUISHED colleague once remarked to me that whatever has been said by Mr. A or Mr. B concerning theory of poetry is simply Mr. A or Mr. B shooting off his mouth. And indeed there seems to be a general agreement that poetry cannot be defined, or that a definition of poetry, if one could be reached, would be of no utility. I do not myself believe that the situation is so desperate if only one will be content with a definition that includes a relative term. The impasse in theory of poetry is not due to any lack of the stuff to be defined nor to any remarkable difficulty in shaping the definition. It is due to a reluctance on the part of human beings to consider the nature of definition itself. The bleak abstractness of definitions of poetry provokes derisive gestures in those who "love stories but hate reasoning." They forget that the usefulness of a definition is generally in direct ratio to its lack of particularity. Suppose that, instead of presenting a definition at the outset and defending it, we consider this and other reasons why definitions of poetry commonly fail to satisfy.

1) *Definitions of poetry are rejected because they are*

not themselves poetical. The majority of readers feel cheated if a definition of poetry does not incite the exalted experience which we associate with the reading of poems. We want to be told that "poetry is a sword of lightning, ever unsheathed, which consumes the scabbard that would contain it," or that "poets are the mirrors of the gigantic shadows which futurity casts upon the present; the trumpets which sing to battle; the unacknowledged legislators of the world." But that insistence is a little naïve. A botanist's definition of a daisy is a very useful thing, and it retains its utility only by declining to do for us what Chaucer and Burns and Wordsworth have done in their poems. The fact is that literary criticism has been cursed by being too literary. The model for a theoretical work is not Shelley's *Defence of Poetry* but Aristotle's *Poetics.*

2) *Definitions of poetry are rejected because they are not formulas or recipes.* The majority of people lose interest in theory of poetry when they are told that it is not concerned with "creative writing" and will not help one in the least to become a poet. But there are many other things besides poetry for which a genetic definition cannot be given. One can buy a blueprint of a house or a locomotive, but not of a daisy.

3) *Definitions of poetry are rejected because they insist on introducing moral judgments prematurely.* It should be apparent that the only definition that stands a chance of being generally acceptable is a "scientific" or naturalistic definition, that is, a description of those features of the object about which people do not quarrel. A great many things could be said about tobacco, but the only way to

begin is as Webster does: "Any solanaceous plant of the genus *Nicotiana,* esp. of the various species cultivated for their leaves, the most common being *N. tabacum,* of South American origin, but no longer known in the wild state. It is a tall annual with ample ovate or lanceolate leaves and white or pink tubular flowers." That is not wildly exciting, but it has the prime characteristic of a basic definition: no one will take exception to it. If, however, you advance the more striking definition "Tobacco is a filthy weed," or with Spenser call it "divine Tobacco," grouping it with panacæa and polygony, you will find agreement, but only in a sect. At the basic level of definition we are not concerned with utility or moral value. And the example of tobacco shows that if we are ever to make any progress, we must agree to recognize several levels in definition. At the first (in our case the aesthetic) level, we should ideally be able to agree. On the other levels we shall certainly divide into mutually exclusive groups. We can agree to a certain extent as to how poetry works, but we shall disagree as to its proper subject matter.

4) *Definitions of poetry fail because they attempt to combine general and specific matter in an arbitrary fashion.* One would not try to define Life in such a way as to include all the distinguishing features of a middle-aged man with a beard and a top hat, who belongs to the Presbyterian Church, has a wife and three children, and votes the Democratic ticket. Yet he is undoubtedly a living organism. If you wish to define Life, you must come down past men and apes, past birds and fishes, past all constructions of living cells even, to protoplasm, the basic chemical substance out of which all living things are made.

The definition of man would contain much that the definition of an ape would not, and vice versa; and in order to find a common denominator for man, ape, lobster, and paramecium you would have to make that denominator as broad and general as protoplasm itself.

People quarrel with definitions of poetry because they do not seem to be specifications of a particular kind of poetry which they happen to approve of. That, again, is a little naïve. It is as though one should condemn a definition of *homo sapiens* on the ground that it does not stipulate that the *homo* should be white. An immense amount of time has been wasted in attempting to handle as general and theoretical what is in fact particular and historical: in attempting definitions of poetry that shall include design, metaphor, meter—the characteristics of particular developed poetries. Poetry, the general, all-embracing term, does not include any of these things in its specifications, any more than Life presupposes hands or a backbone.

5) *Definitions of poetry fail because they try to make absolute and objective what is in fact conventional and empirical.* The protoplasm with which theory of poetry deals is human speech—all of it, all the time. Every time a man speaks aloud, every time he silently formulates thought into words, he is engaged in an aesthetic activity; that is, he is a poet. As theorists we can analyze the uses of language into two: we can say that there is a "scientific" or "prose" use of language, and an "aesthetic" or "poetic" use of language. I *shall* say just that later on. The point to insist on here is that in actual speech the two never occur separately. To obtain "pure prose" (that is,

prose with no expressive or poetic quality) we should have to resort to mathematical symbols. To obtain "pure poetry" (that is, poetry with no trace of practical information) we should have to resort to music. Neither would be human speech. All human speech is basically of a kind, as all living organisms are protoplasm. All human speech is poetry. The difference between the baldest freshman theme and *Hamlet*—and there is a great difference—is one of degree, not one of kind.

Of course when we use the word poetry in ordinary discourse, we do not mean anything so ubiquitous. We mean that kind of speech in which the expressive or poetic predominates greatly over the information-giving, or practical, or prose element. Rigorous analysis and rigid terminology will never fix a point which is in fact shifting. And if the placing of the dividing line between prose and poetry (in the popular sense of the term) is more or less arbitrary—if it depends upon an individual empirical judgment as to whether, on the whole, the expressive or the practical predominates—then all definitions which pretend to place that line absolutely and objectively will fail to satisfy.

Let us begin our definition by cutting in two (if you prefer hard words, say "recognizing the dichotomy in") the word "good" as applied to poetry. "Good" poetry may mean either "poetry that is good art" or "poetry that is good for you"; and they are not necessarily the same thing. It would, for many reasons, be comforting to believe that the superior expressiveness of *Paradise Lost* is directly due to the superior moral profundity of Milton, but the principle when applied to cases generally calls for so much qualification as to prove it nugatory. We must explicitly separate the critical judgment into two judgments: the aesthetic and the moral, or, as Tolstoi said, into "judgment of art considered apart from subject matter" and "judgment according to subject matter." Poetry is good in the aesthetic sense (is good as art) when it is expressive and infectious: when the poet, contemplating an experience, has succeeded in finding verbal equivalents for it which enable another person to build an experience in *his* mind which is (as we suppose) recognizably like the artist's in quality, and not too much inferior to it in intensity. That the experience of the artist may be vicious makes no difference in the first judgment. Goodness or usefulness is no part of the basic definition of art. And if you are talking about poetry as something to be distinguished from other things, expressiveness is of much greater importance than goodness. A group of words may be expressive and moral, in which case it is poetry, and poetry of a particularly valuable kind; or it may be moral but not expressive, in which case, though it may be admirable morality, it is not poetry at all. Moral profundity may add value to what is expressed, but it cannot in any way make up for expressive weakness.

Romantic aesthetic made poetry the highest activity of the human mind, "Reason in her most exalted mood." Poetry was thought of as a superior way of apprehending Truth, as the apex of the pyramid of the mind. We shall find many difficulties avoided if we turn from this esoteric conception of art, identify poetry with language itself, and thus open our eyes to its ubiquity and its primitive nature. Let us, in short, reverse the order of the layers of the pyramid and make poetry not the apex, but the base. Poetry is not a higher kind of reason; it is the first grade of verbalized experience, prior to logic, prior to morality. The world (whatever is outside ourselves) makes its impression on us. Our minds impose human form on this matter, grasp it intuitively. I do not use the word in a mystical sense; I mean simply that the action which I have called "grasping" is unanalyzable. It is unanalyzable because it is already simpler than anything else. There has somewhere to be a first step, and this is it. The mind *expresses* its intuitions in verbal symbols, and that expression is poetry. Why certain sounds should serve better than others to express a given intuition is a mystery, but in every construction of thought something has to be left mysterious as a condition of making a beginning at all. Poetry is not merely words printed in books or recited from a stage; it is just as much poetry if it consists of words held in consciousness but never uttered. During all the moments of our waking or dreaming life we are engaged in the poetic activity.

But most of us are not engaged in poetic activity of any degree of intensity. There are degrees of expressive power: degrees of vividness, of coherence, of complexity. An electric current circulates in all of us, but the poets are men of terrific voltage. Only when we judge that a certain voltage has been attained do we bother in common parlance to call a man a poet.

But there is another activity of the mind. Our intuitions (the poetical content of our minds) are non-reflective, individual, and particular. The mind is also constantly

engaged in the business of identifying, sorting, and classi-
fying them with a view to possible action. Some theorists
feel it necessary to be very subtle in defining the non-
aesthetic activities of the mind; for example, to differentiate the logical and the scientific sharply from the practical.
I find that I can get on nicely by lumping everything that
is distinct from the aesthetic, and calling it indifferently
the utilitarian, the practical, the scientific. However you
name this side of the mind's activity, it is opposed to the
poetic. In theory, it could be utterly free from poetry, but
not in practice, for if it speaks, it must use words, and
words can never be divested utterly of their expressive or
poetic power. The most austere scientific treatise occasionally startles us by its unintended poetry. But in general
if the practical activity predominates, the poetical quality
of language will be so much diluted as not to be noticed.

We must remind ourselves that the analysis which we
have just been making is in the highest degree theoretical and abstract. The activity of the human mind is in
fact a unit and a continuum. There is not in it a succession of aesthetic and practical moments. The two are like
Aristotle's Form and Matter, which can be thought of separately but do not exist independently, unless it be in
heaven. Reality lies in the complex and unanalyzed activity of the mind, but we cannot talk about that reality
without breaking it up into smaller and simpler units. The
units are, admittedly, fictions, but it is the fate of all
analysis of the mind to deal in fictions. All that I really
wish to make clear is that what we call poetry must be
seen, not as something occult and esoteric, but as portions of verbal experience detaching themselves from the

background of ordinary speech because of their greater richness and intensity.

Richness: does it not follow from this that there *is* a direct connection between moral and intellectual profundity and poetic creativeness? The answer, I still think, is no. The unusual degree of expressive power which causes a man to be recognized as a poet is his by grace of God (*poeta nascitur*), and it is not increased by the strenuous discipline through which he acquires wisdom and virtue. Indeed, since the activity mainly concerned in the acquirement of wisdom and virtue is the non-poetical or anti-poetical, there is a real chance that a discipline leading to wisdom and virtue will be accompanied by a decline in expressive power. Nearly all children are artistic, many college students have a distinct poetic gift, almost all adults have got safely over it. But if a man highly gifted with the childlike faculty of expressiveness can retain it while he acquires intellectual and moral profundity, his intuitions will naturally be more rich, complex, and valuable than those coming from a man of inferior intellectual and moral grasp. Not all good and wise men are poets; not all poets are good and wise men; but a good and wise man who is a poet is a particularly valuable kind of poet.

What do I mean by language that is "expressive"? It is language that makes us more sharply conscious of experience as experience, language which gives us the immediate *qualities* of experience, instead of indicating its *uses*. The greater part of an adult mental life is preoccupied by the business of making a living:

> The world is too much with us; late and soon
> Getting and spending, we lay waste our powers.

67

"Getting and spending," not merely in the gross and obvious sense of making money, but of all those strivings of the mind to interpret the experiences in which we are immersed, so as to wrest them to our advantage. From the serene constructions of the theoretical physicist to the anxious endeavor to pay the rent, the mind ranges in its task of "making sense" of naïve experience; that is, of identifying its parts and arranging them for immediate or possible action. But naïve experience is still possible. Life comes to us full of qualities of color and smell and taste and sound and touch: of unreasonable passion and useless excitement. It comes with a fullness of qualities far beyond anything that our practical needs demand. We know that it is good for us to realize life in this uncalculating mood of fullness, and we do realize it when we can succeed in keeping our attention on it. When we are successful, we enjoy a state of *heightened consciousness*, something very different from the state of mind which is commonly ours as we plod along on our purposive way, conscious but no more conscious than we can help. But it is very difficult to hold this state of heightened consciousness against the consuming restlessness of the mind to identify experience, to classify it for purposes of action. The moment the mind reverts to this activity, the heightened consciousness vanishes. That is, as soon as we have satisfactorily identified a bit of experience for present or future use, we lose the qualities of the experience, for they slide out of the area of our consciousness.

"We can dress ourselves from top to toe [says Max Eastman] without once consciously perceiving a limb or a garment, provided the garments are in their proper place, and the limbs too, and all goes well. But if something obstructs the process—if an arm will not pass through the sleeve of a coat—then that situation automatically swims into our ken. Or suppose it has been dimly in our ken, it becomes more sharply so. It swims into the focus of attention. And as it does so the sleeve which our arm will not pass through becomes, let us say, a hole in the lining of our coat. As soon as we have perceived the experience in this way—and perhaps inwardly named it *torn lining*—the process of dressing is resumed with a correction, and may now go through to the end without further intrusion from the mind. I think that is a fair example of how consciousness arises, or is heightened, in practical life. And that use of the words, torn lining, in order to resolve a situation that was in doubt and enable us to resume an obstructed activity, is typical of the practical or prose use of words. It shows how practical words, in their simple and original function, not only do not heighten consciousness, but reduce it and get rid of it."

What poetry demands is *impractical* identifications. We call them metaphors. "*Any* impractical identification that you can induce somebody to listen to is poetic, because it is the essence of an attentive consciousness. It is mind suspended on the brink of action."

Prosaisms in poetry would appear to be uncompromisingly practical identifications. Is not this the real source of the uneasiness we feel in reading the original version of Wordsworth's *Thorn?*

> High on a mountain's highest ridge,
> Where oft the stormy winter gale

Cuts like a scythe, while through the clouds
It sweeps from vale to vale;
Not five yards from the mountain-path,
This thorn you on your left espy;
And to the left, three yards beyond,
You see a little muddy pond
Of water, never dry;
I've measured it from side to side:
'Tis three feet long, and two feet wide.

I will not say that this is not poetry, for I think on the whole it is; only that it is very hard to hold the heightened consciousness of the wild wind-swept ridge so powerfully expressed in the first part of the stanza against the assault of the enumeration in the second part. The trouble is not that "three feet long, and two feet wide" is vulgar or low—the contemporary objection; it is rather that such anxious attention to exact mensuration ("I've *measured* it from side to side") is normally the mark of a mind interested in the uses of objects rather than their qualities, of a man talking prose rather than poetry. Nor are the objections removed by Wordsworth's long note assuring us that the poem is dramatic: that he is not speaking in his own person but in that of a retired sea-captain, a person who may be presumed to be credulous and talkative. The defense would be irresistible if he had added that of course he meant the poem to be in places dull and ludicrous, which he does not do. On the contrary, his remark that he conceived the whole as "impregnated with passion" shows that he thought he had attained a uniformly poetic effect. He did not enjoy the dramatic gift in any high degree, and *The Thorn* is one of the doctrinaire poems of 1798, written to prove his theory of poetic diction. Either of these causes may have been operating when he decided that a man engaged in applying a yardstick might be "in a state of vivid sensation." In any case, general experience has shown that a reader who comes to the lines without prejudice will suffer, as Coleridge aptly says, a "sudden and unpleasant sinking." Compare the doubtful success of those lines with the unquestionable success of these:

> Ten thousand saw I at a glance,
> Tossing their heads in sprightly dance.

If ten thousand is a more poetical number than three or two (and I think it is), it is not because there is any difference between genuine numbers, but because a man who says "ten thousand" is not commonly suspected of having counted. If Wordsworth had said something here like "I've measured it from side to side," that is, if he had given us to understand that he had counted the daffodils and that there were just exactly ten thousand, no more, no less, "Ten thousand saw I at a glance" would be as bad as " 'Tis three feet long and two feet wide." But he did not. He did not count at all. He was merely expressing by an impractical enumeration one of the most prominent qualities of the experience: "What quantities of them! How close together!"

Poetic language is language that expresses the qualities of experience, as distinguished from language that indicates its uses. Since all language is to some extent expressive in this sense, all human speech is, strictly speaking, poetry in various degrees of concentration. *In the ordinary or popular sense of the term, poetry is language in which expression of the qualities of experience is felt to predominate greatly over statement concerning its uses.*

But we must not forget what we have said about sensibility and shifts of sensibility. The qualities of experience are neither perceived nor expressed in the same way by different organizations of sensibility. At the very lowest level of consciousness a selective process is operating (I have already used the analogy of a radio receiving set), and the mechanism of that process is what I have called basis of sensibility. Experimental psychology has demonstrated conclusively that human minds are very far from being passive instruments which perceive in the same way when faced by identical situations. At the very lowest level we can reach to, a process of evaluation is going on. We do not hear all the sounds that impinge on our ear drums; we hear what we are listening for. We do not see all the objects mirrored by our retinas; we see what we are looking for. We hear and see, in short, in terms of our interests; and our supposed perception is to a lesser or greater extent inference. A shift in sensibility means ultimately the perception of a different world. Our definition therefore contains an ambiguous or relative term: an ambiguity or relativity which it was the purpose of my first two lectures to show to be inevitable. Though the addition, strictly speaking, creates a tautology, it may be safer if we say, "Poetic language is language that expresses the qualities of experience *in terms of a given sensibility*."

Mr. Eastman, from whom I have taken so many of my terms, talks both of the "qualities of experience" and the "qualities of things," phrases which he clearly considers interchangeable. No doubt in properly controlled terminology they are interchangeable. But in a popular discourse such as this, I am afraid of defining poetry as that kind of speech which expresses the qualities of *things*, because I should almost certainly be understood as saying that speech cannot be poetical unless it deals with the qualities of concrete objects. I regard as a Romantic heresy the common assumption of our time that the concrete and individual are essentially poetical and that the general is unpoetic. The heightened consciousness which is the mark of poetry may result either from an awareness of individual concrete objects or of generalized objects. Whether it results from one or the other will depend upon the basis of sensibility. One can have a heightened consciousness of Man as well as of a man; of "leaden death" as well as of a bullet. Generalization is not the opposite of poetry, but practical identification is.

To the majority of people this definition of poetry will be repugnant for at least three reasons: It leaves out all the marks by which poetry, in the popular sense of the term, is distinguished: that is, meter, rhyme, metaphor, simile, plot, and all the others. It seems to contain no explanation of that transport, that sudden glorious illumination and elevation which Longinus advances as the prime criterion of poetry. And it seems to be morally irresponsible.

Aristotle, the first and greatest of the formalists, will support me against the first objection. You will remember that he defined poetry as "imitation of action" or "imitation of men in action," and resolutely refused to admit meter in his prime definition. He admitted it later when he defined Tragedy, for the ample reason that, as a matter of simple historical observation, he found it in the trage- dies accessible to him. It would not be proper, however, to claim the protection of Aristotle any further. He was not only a formalist but an absolutist. Having collected representative specimens of Greek poetry, he divided them into *genres* (epic, drama, lyric, etc.), and then analyzed each genre for the typical or ideal form. The method was precisely that which he had employed in biology, and he seems really to have felt that the typical form of tragedy which he described had the same kind of general and en- during validity as his description of the type specimen of a fish. That is, though his basic definition of poetry excludes the concept of determinate form, the essential character of tragedy is assumed to reside in a union and interaction of formal elements (meter, plot, character, "intellectual element," etc.) and those formal elements are assumed to describe adequately not only the tragedies of the past but also those of the future. I have come reluctantly to the con- clusion that Aristotle was guilty of a fallacy when he concluded that a method of description proper for natural organisms reproducing their own kind could be applied in anything but an analogical sense to mental constructions like tragedies, but my respect for his analysis of *Greek* tragedy is not thereby lessened. Remove the metaphysics from the Aristotelian method and make it genuinely his- torical (that is, relativistic), and it seems to me the best of all methods. I am as much a formalist as anybody if you do not insist on the absolute and permanent validity of your forms. I think we would all agree that the best part of the experience of a poem is intuitive; is mainly direct, unreflecting, and unconscious of parts. But when we an-

74

alyze that experience (and we must analyze it to talk about it), I know of no better way than to point to its *structure*. It is only when the structure of Greek tragedy as discerned by Aristotle is made a measure of the excellence of Shakespeare, or Romantic poetry is judged by norms derived from the analysis of Modern and Metaphysical poetry, that I demur. It is not formalism I object to but absolutism.

To state the basic definition in terms of the effect produced by all poetry on the human mind is not to deny that any particular specimen you may care to advance can be analyzed for formal qualities capable of producing the effect. Alliteration, assonance, rhyme, parallelism, even meter, must certainly be excluded as essentials of a general definition, for it is possible to cite highly developed poetry that lacks one or more of them. Plot and metaphor go much deeper, and indeed, if you will stretch the terms far enough, go to the very bottom. We have seen that impractical identifications are essential to the kind of speech that heightens consciousness. It is clear, too, that in order to heighten consciousness the sounds employed must be, in part at least, intelligible: they must be real words, capable of arousing ideas, or they must suggest real words. Poetic speech must, in short, have *some* "meaning." If, then, you will stretch the word "plot" to include every meaningful arrangement of language and "metaphor" to cover every use of speech that gives us the qualities of experience, you can work out a formal basic definition that will include plot and metaphor. I myself find little utility in the application to such inchoate material of technical terms invented to describe highly developed forms of poetry. When so used the terms seem to me figurative and fanciful—like saying that the amoeba has a mouth and a stomach because it ingests food, or that it has fins because it propels itself through the water. There is little danger that we shall underestimate the importance of formal elements in poetry, but there is real danger that through preoccupation with them we shall lose our sense of the basic continuity of expressive speech.

I should not like to be understood as saying that the formal elements of poetry are mere conventional and adventitious wrappings imposed on something that would still be in their absence the kind of poetry that it is. Poetry begins logically with a form as simple and inchoate as that of the amoeba, and builds up to forms as complicated and particular as that of man. When we instance the formal elements of developed poetry—plot, meter, rhyme, alliteration, assonance, and all the rest—we are dealing not with externals but with the particularity of the poem. Croce is right in saying that the only judgment you can make about poetry *qua* poetry is that it exists, but that does not mean that you cannot differentiate particular poems. If "alive" means merely "animate, not dead," then an amoeba is as much alive as a man, though it has no backbone, no hands, no feet, no ears, no eyes, no stomach, and no heart. But if "alive" means "aware of existence in a very complicated way and able to cope with it in a very resourceful manner," then a man is much more alive than an amoeba. In the same way poetry of more complicated structure is, or ought to be, more poetical than that kind which reaches to the bare boundary of form.

Start, then, with the basic definition, and add as many historical *differentiae* as are necessary for distinguishing the body of poetry in question. If you insist on becoming more particular, you will find your definitions becoming chapters of literary history. There is no definition of Shakespeare's poetry short of the complete poetical works of Shakespeare and a variorum commentary.

The greatest value to criticism of our basic definition is that it does insist on what I have called the continuity of expressive language. In a fine article published in the *Atlantic Monthly* not long ago, Mr. Edmund Wilson spoke of the sterility which much of our contemporary criticism (particularly academic criticism) courts by identifying poetry with verse. Two hundred—even one hundred—years ago verse was the accepted medium for a great body of imaginative writing which this age would unhesitatingly put in prose. That does not mean that Pope was wrong in writing imaginative philosophical essays in verse, or that Scott would have done better to write *The Lady of the Lake* in prose. Nor does it mean that poetry is withering. It means that the specifications of poetry have changed. Our greatest poet today may be, as Mr. Wilson thinks, a novelist: Joyce. If this view were accepted, the consequences in our formal teaching of English literature would be considerable. Is it not clear that our preoccupation with metered writing is excessive? If one wishes to find the real counterpart of the dramatic genius of Shakespeare in the early nineteenth century, he will not find it in the verse dramas of Coleridge, Byron, and Shelley, but in the novels of Walter Scott. Yet the major works of Scott are less studied in college classes than the minor works of Shelley—and simply because Shelley's writings are in verse.

It is not strange that the feeling of transport or illumination which accompanies the poetic experience should have caused people to believe that poetry speaks Truth in a higher sense than the discourse of rational inquiry. Truth attained by rational inquiry seems generally a tame thing as compared with the immediate illumination of great poetry. And naturally, since the experience of poetry is so valuable, man wishes to find a fitting sanction for it. But does it logically follow that poetry is therefore "higher" if by "higher" is meant that it calls into play a more refined and difficult exercise of the mental faculties? I think not. Rational inquiry is tame as compared with poetry because we proceeded by conscious steps to the result, and know how we got there. In poetry we know of no intermediate steps, because there were none. The mysterious urgency of poetry is not due to its being more complex and civilized than reason, but rather to its being more uncivilized, primitive, and simple. Poetry is the first motion of the mind into language, the direct, unanalyzable intuition.

Our definition would be morally irresponsible if we said that a man should or could rest indefinitely in the aesthetic mode. I share the irritation of all serious men with those imperfect followers of Croce who talk as though the intrusion of the problem of morality into a discussion of literary theory were a profanation. To maintain that we ought to leave moral judgments alone in our first approach to art is not to deny the necessity of making such judgments; it is simply to say that we are not in a very good position to ask the question, "Is this experience worth spending my time on?" or "Is this experience good for me?" until we are sure that we know what the experience *is*. For art is experience, and man as a moral being is surely under the necessity of subjecting *all* his experiences to moral evaluation. No moralistic critic can be more uncompromising than I in stating the fundamental assumption that it is more important that I be a good man than that I be able to tell a good poem when I see it.

In a system which accepts sensibility as a starting point, there does not appear to be much utility in subtle analysis of the causes of aesthetic value. That is aesthetically valuable which expresses a sensibility—any sensibility. Heightened consciousness is always and under all circumstances a positive value. If we decline to accept it, or disapprove of it having accepted it, it is because it is incompatible with some other value which we prefer. Since the general basis of sensibility which we have attributed to each age is an abstraction arrived at by historical study of the average or prevailing characteristics of a large group of individuals who actually show considerable differences from one another, we should not expect at any time to find complete agreement as to aesthetic value any more than (to state in different terms what is fundamentally the same problem) we should expect to find complete agreement as to what constitutes good English style, or even correct English usage. We shall always be conscious of our differences from our fellows, leaving it for the future historian to find that we were so much alike that he can hardly tell us apart. There is no compulsion upon any person to share the aesthetic values of another. We may well suspect that if the person who claims such values is a contemporary

79

and is otherwise shown to be sane and sensitive, our failure to find the values he reports is due to impatience or ignorance, and humble ourselves accordingly. If we stubbornly refuse to share the accepted taste of the group in which we move, we shall certainly make ourselves subject to social reprisals. But there are no ethics of taste. Crudity in poetic judgment is no more wicked than crudity in grammar. The determination to make moral soundness the test of aesthetic validity is today strong in two groups of critics. In one it is the result of an attempt to substitute poetry for dogma. It is the mark of a religious nature which has lost faith in a dogmatic theology and is striving to find a substitute. This group has complacently accepted moral relativism but shrinks from giving up all fixities. The other group consists of earnest theologians who fear the consequences of admitting the principle of relativism anywhere in the analysis of what they denominate the things of the spirit. Both groups, as it seems to me, are not merely more concerned about morals and theology than about poetry (which is right), but are also convinced that morals and theology will go to pot if it is admitted that poetry can in a real sense be good without being wise. In this I think that they are too timid. The cause of morals and theology will be strengthened, not weakened, if they are not forced to defend areas in which they are at a disadvantage.

I am well aware of the logical difficulties involved in this separation of the aesthetic and the moral judgments. Poetry consists of words and nothing else. You cannot read it once for aesthetic value, ignoring the meaning of the words, and then read it again for moral content, ignoring its aesthetic value. It does seem to be true that what may be called the mechanical features of its formal pattern elicit in us a definite physiological response that is quite innocent of thought. Read *The Destruction of Sennacherib* or the chorus from *Atalanta in Calydon* to a man who did not know a word of English and you would soon set him listening for the recurrence of the rhymes and beating time:

> Ta ta *tum* ta ta *tum* ta ta *tum* ta ta *tum*.

But though this may be a very compelling *background* for a state of heightened consciousness, it is *in itself* about as remote from heightened consciousness as anything that one can suggest. A man can let his mind go woolgathering during a concert and beat time with his foot for minutes on end without knowing it. In order to make us more keenly aware of the qualities of experience the patterns of stress and sound must be associated with meanings, or rather, must come to us through meanings. Not necessarily clear meanings or the meanings the poet intended. We can get intense pleasure out of the first stanza of the *Chorus*—

> And the brown bright nightingale amorous
> Is half assuaged for Itylus,
> For the Thracian ships and the foreign faces,
> The tongueless vigil, and all the pain—

without knowing the myth of Philomela. But none of the phrases which seem especially delightful to us—say "tongueless vigil"—would cause any particular excitement if we did not know what "tongue" meant and were not willing to make a guess at "vigil."

Aesthetic value, then, is not the perception of some sort

of "music" woven into the words of poetry but detachable from them. It is heightened consciousness enjoyed for its own sake—the whole rich tissue of a poem held as an object of pure contemplation without any intrusion of the practical will. The poem, considered as an instrument, is not two things. But the *experience* of the poem can be held in a state of detachment and disinterestedness, or we can proceed to assimilate it to our practical natures.

Taste is a matter of contemplation; morals concern action. Evil into the mind of god or man may come and go, as Adam told Eve, but it is only as a man's will approves that he is subject to moral censure. We are all agreed, I fancy, that there are dangerous books. Eve committed no sin in enjoying the wicked dream, but all the same the dream made it easier for her to pluck the apple. We should probably find on comparing notes that our views of the moral harmfulness of particular books tended to be relative: that, as Andrew Lang says somewhere, there are stories which should be read only by Arabs and old gentlemen. But censorship of some sort is as necessary in theory as it has been constant in practice.

The crux in all censorship, public and private, is that in the vast majority of cases we do not know what the connection is between aesthetic experience and either religious faith or moral behavior. And since we are still puzzled after so long a study of the problem, it is not likely that we shall ever know. What does seem to be clear, however, is that the ideas, the doctrine, of a genuine work of art are of secondary importance as compared with its images, and that both suffer remarkable changes when taken into a mind already formed by miscellaneous experience. *A priori* it would have to be argued, I think, that extensive reading of Shelley at an early age might be dangerous to faith and even to morals. But I have to testify that my own reading of Shelley (which occurred in my twentieth year), though it possessed me with the strength of a conversion and led me into ridiculous postures of identification with my idol, served, unless I am greatly mistaken, as the first stage in a conversion to orthodox Christianity. Shelley's poems seemed to me to burst the flimsy barriers of my previous narrow world, and to leave me whirling in giddy rapture amidst great new masses of almost intolerably vivid mental stuff which finally settled into that very configuration which Shelley most detested.

Wordsworth, we are told, subscribed in his earlier poems to the Hartleian doctrine that our moral nature is built up from the images with which our brain is stocked. "The language of the sense," he says, "is

> The anchor of my purest thoughts, the nurse,
> The guide, the guardian of my heart, and soul
> Of all my *moral* being."

Croce, in our own time, has maintained what amounts to the same thing. The aesthetic faculty, he would say, is not something to which we turn to soften and decorate the austere workings of the reason (the eighteenth-century heresy); rather, the aesthetic faculty furnishes the logical faculty all the materials it ever has to work with. And the same would be true of our moral nature. Good deeds are better than good poems, but without poems (in the wider sense) there could be no good deeds. There is something profoundly true in this. No one, in my opinion, is often in a position to predict with any degree of confidence what the final effect of a work of art will be on another's moral character. And Puritanism, which is the heavy-handed suppression in the interests of righteousness of all that does not seem to be directly moral, is shown by history to have introduced as many evils as it has eliminated.

There is no way to escape the burden of casuistry. Each of us knows what he can eat and what he had better leave alone; and each of us, if he is at all given to self-examination, has a pretty good notion whether his moral digestion will stand a given book or not. We protect children from books that might cause trouble, as we keep certain kinds of food from them, but when they grow up they must decide by the testimony of their own livers and their own consciences. It was profoundly said by St. Augustine that all morality can be summed up in the injunction, "Love God, and do what you will." The saying could as well take the form, "Love God, and read what you will."

But perhaps I have been restricting my discussion of the judgment according to subject matter too narrowly to its reflection of the morals of the poet and the effect which his poem may have on the morals of the reader. There is a more inclusive consideration which is theoretically of even greater importance: the *knowledge* and experience of the poet. Can there be a valuable expression of subject matter that is nonsensical, banal, trivial, childish, eccentric, or perverse?

The different categories demand separate treatment. It is clear from what has already been said that there can be no valuable expression of nonsense, if nonsense is taken to mean that which is completely unintelligible. Poetry is language, and language by definition is intelligible. The nonsense verses of a Carroll or a Lear are not nonsense; they consist either of a series of logical *non-sequiturs*, or their invented "nonsense" words occur in a context of words that are intelligible.

Banality presents a more subtle problem. When in the prose or practical world we call a statement banal, we do not mean that it may not be clearly phrased or that it is not true or important. We mean rather that it is so much a matter of common knowledge that the person addressed could have made it as well as the speaker, and the speaker (to quote Wordsworth) is suspected of having adopted it or spoken it by rote. It is impossible to give valuable expression to this kind of banality because it is not poetically felt. But there is no truism so flat or banal that, to quote Wordsworth again, it cannot be perceived in its whole compass with the freshness and clearness of an original intuition. If a man has *experienced* a truism and can find language to express the qualities of that experience, the result may be poetry of the greatest distinction. When we say that a piece of verse is banal, we do not or should not mean that the author's subject matter was so commonplace that he could not give it valuable expression. We do or should mean either that he had no real *poetic* subject matter, or that he was clumsy in expressing it. An insistence that the "message" of a poem, when abstracted and given prose formulation, shall be novel or exciting would throw out of court nearly all the poems in the *Golden Treasury*. Can any one rephrase the most famous of the Lucy poems in practical speech and obtain anything but a banality?

This analysis shows us how careful we must be when we consider the term "trivial." I have assumed that a banality may be a true and important statement of general human experience. A trivial subject matter, in the prose sense, is presumably one which, whether true or not, is of little or no practical importance. If, when you ask the question, you are extending the term to *poetic* subject matter, you have already answered your question by begging it. A trivial poetic subject matter can be expressed and the expression will be valuable, but of trifling value. Human speech is filled with poetic value of this sort. What is really meant by the question is whether it is possible to experience significantly in terms of quality matter which general practical sense regards as trifling. And the answer is that it *is* possible. In the first place, "trivial" is a highly relative term: it means "trifling as compared with something else." No intelligible statement or view of things is under all circumstances void of importance. Trifles have a way of becoming tremendous. A trifle may be the cause of poetic excitement by suddenly becoming practically important. And in the second place there is a kind of poetry in which trifles become highly significant to the poet though he remains quite conscious of the fact that they are practically unimportant, and indeed shares that view himself. Such poetry is usually gay, airy, and irresponsible, but I do not know that it has to be. Swift's preoccupation with filth may be another illustration.

But the poet who deals with matter which the general practical sense of mankind regards as trivial, childish, eccentric, or perverse has to pay for it. If poetry is not at bottom a criticism of life, it is tested as criticism of life before most critics are done with it. If we can get two values, we prefer them to one. Granted (so far as we can tell by the evidence of our nerves) that two poets give us the same amount of aesthetic value, we are bound in the long run to prefer that one whose experience of life is deeper, whose doctrines seem to us more serious, mature, and true. Man is fundamentally a serious animal and a soul with a serious destiny: he cannot, and should not, remain exclusively in the state of contemplation. We do not have to accept the doctrines of a poem in order to enjoy it as poetry, but if its doctrines seem to us true, we shall certainly find the experience of reading it more valuable than that of reading one which presents doctrines which we consider childish or false.

This sounds like mere arithmetic, but in practice it is not so simple. It is commonly said that "other things being equal" we prefer the poem with the sounder subject matter. But there is no certain way of knowing that other things are equal. Our measures of aesthetic value are variables whose changes cannot be estimated. And there is no common measure of aesthetic value and what for short I call moral value. The total critical act of evaluation is a compromise. I will allow an unparalleled offering of aesthetic value to make up for a comparative weakness of moral value (*The Ancient Mariner, Christabel*); I will allow sincerity and strength of message to make up for coarseness of expressive technique (*Childe Harold* III). Others will strike their balances differently, and I do not see on what grounds either of us is to be called wrong. Who can say what the units should be, and how many units of one should balance how many units of the other?

I do not need to point out that the empirical and personal nature of this balancing of values is another argument for a relativistic theory of poetry. Entering into all our judgments of aesthetic value is a variable, the basis of sensibility; and the final summation of values cannot be made with reference to any objective standard.

The critical judgment is not one, but two. It properly deals with other things than poetry. We ought perhaps now to say something of the pure article.

V

PURE POETRY IN THEORY
AND PRACTICE

Poetry, we have said, is that kind of speech which expresses the qualities of experience. It is, speaking strictly and theoretically, coextensive with language. Speaking popularly, it occurs when the concentration of the expressive element of speech becomes so great that we distinctly feel it to predominate over that other element which we have called the practical or scientific. But suppose the concentration is carried to the point of eliminating the non-poetic altogether? What, in short, of pure poetry? Is there such a thing? If it exists, is it a good thing?

Modern theory of poetry is very much preoccupied with these questions, whereas older theory of poetry seems not to have been bothered with them at all. We may therefore suspect that our theoretical interest is a reflection of some inner tension to which our age is peculiarly subject. In the book to which I referred in my last lecture, Mr. Eastman dwells at length on the conflict between the scientific and the literary spirit, and draws some very discouraging conclusions as to the future of the profession of letters. Poetry as a conscious art began, he thinks, in sheer magic and incantation, but, very early, poets were persuaded by public adulation and their own vanity to consider themselves seers. They set themselves up as retailers of a more essential Truth than could ever be attained or uttered by the meddling intellect. But science has been steadily demolishing their claim to any regard on this score. Every time they have set a boundary beyond which science was not to pass, science has proceeded to march in and take over. The field of poetry, he maintains, is steadily shrinking, and must continue to shrink until it coincides with the poet's proper domain. Poets and critics must come to realize that the poet, as a poet, does not reveal truth to us, or perform any directly practical service whatever. The "truths" to which he commits himself prove in retrospect no more enduring than the "truths" of the scientists, but his work possesses a currency denied to theirs. That is because he gives us the qualities of experience in states of heightened consciousness.

Mr. Ransom also has considered this assault upon the poets, and has analyzed its causes, as I think, more profoundly. The determination to separate poetry from science is only one aspect of the thoroughgoing tendency of the modern mind to analyze everything. When our descendants of the next century seek for an epithet with which to damn our times, they might well choose something like "The Era of Purity." Our present-day Puritanism (the culmination of a tendency going at least as far back as the Reformation) is not content with a demand for pure poetry and pure science; it yearns also for pure religion, pure politics, pure food, and pure business. The modern temper disapproves of the amateur and thinks everything had better be turned over to the expert. Consequently we have science without poetry and poetry without science; and we have also Protestantism, republicanism, vitamin pellets, and Mr. Henry Ford. We have split the rich monism of the Age of Innocence up into many separate compartments, and insist on living in each of them by turns.

Coleridge, who has somewhere or other said almost everything that is interesting in theory of poetry, no doubt adumbrated the doctrine of pure poetry in his remark that "a poem of any length neither can be, or ought to be, all poetry," but it was certainly in Poe's hands that the doctrine took shape and acquired power. As Percy's *Reliques* went to Germany and came back in the Gothic ballads of Monk Lewis and Walter Scott, so Poe's pronouncements, largely unheeded in America and England, were developed in France by Baudelaire, Verlaine, Mallarmé, and Valéry, to return to English poetry through the precept and example of Mr. Pound and Mr. Eliot. Poe's views are pretty well known, but we had better recapitulate them. His most famous heresy, reiterated in article after article, is that of the "single sitting"—a long poem, he says, "is simply a flat contradiction in terms." *Paradise Lost* is poetical when regarded "merely as a series of minor poems"; or, more exactly, as a series of short poems embedded in prose. Plot, the *sine qua non* of Aristotle, is not an essential of drama; the most that can be said for it is that "it is but a secondary and rigidly artistical merit, for which no merit of a higher class—no merit founded in nature—should be sacrificed." Poe derives these notions from his belief that poetry deserves the name only when it excites, and all excitements are necessarily transient. Poetry is antithetic to truth, which "has no sympathy with the myrtles." Poetry is the hand-maiden of Taste, as Passion is the handmaiden of the moral sense, and Truth of the intellect; and Truth and Passion are "far more readily attainable in prose." If they are introduced into poetry, it is only to "serve in elucidation, or aid the general effect, as do discords in music, by contrast."

Coleridge, you will recall, said that a poem ought not to be all poetry, and Poe admitted that passion and truth might be profitably introduced into a poem, but his statements invite the conclusion that the more a poet can divest his compositions of everything that is not essentially po-etical, the better the product will be. Certainly that is the conclusion that the modern mind unquestionably draws. If a thing is pure, of course we want it.

But it is only the *preoccupation* with pure poetry that is modern, for the article has always existed. Mr. George Moore has compiled an anthology of pure poems, with specimens going as far back as Skelton. His selections are defined as poems "born of admiration of the only perma-nent world, the world of things," poems "unsicklied o'er with the pale cast of thought," or simply as poems "con-taining no hint of subjectivity." This is not too precise, but that a real principle of selection was operative is shown by the anthology itself, which is remarkably unified in tone. Characteristic choices are Shakespeare's songs, lyrics from Blake's *Songs of Innocence*, and a good deal of Shelley and Poe. Delightful as the volume is, the selection does not seem to me to provide a sufficiently broad basis for a theoretical discussion of the term "pure poetry." On the side of metrical form, Moore is very conservative. And he seems to have had no pleasure in truly modern verse, for the latest poem in the volume is Swinburne's chorus from *Atalanta in Calydon*. My notions of "pure poetry" would not be satisfied by any definition that excluded the Imagists or the modern "obscure" poets.

There are all shades of distinction in "pure poetry," but I find it useful to lump all the varieties under two headings. There is the kind of poetry which is pure because it resolutely refrains from criticism of life, and gives the reader to understand that the intrusion of a moral, or indeed of a conclusion, would be an impertinence. It is always productive of a mood, but it produces the mood directly: it does not say, "Because of these things you ought to be merry or sad." I have indicated several examples from Mr. Moore. Mr. Eastman has added Keats's *Ode to Autumn* as a supreme example of this kind of composition. It "says absolutely nothing throughout thirty-three lines except just this one very thing—Autumn." Another fine example from a poet who is generally credited with little pure poetry is Wordsworth's extempore of April 16, 1802, quite properly labeled at its publication in 1807 "Mood of My Own Mind," though later forced into the more ambitious classification of "Poems of the Imagination." I quote only half of it, but the second stanza is equally innocent of criticism of life:

> The Cock is crowing,
> The stream is flowing,
> The small birds twitter,
> The lake doth glitter,
> The green field sleeps in the sun;
> The oldest and youngest
> Are at work with the strongest;
> The cattle are grazing,

> Their heads never raising;
> There are forty feeding like one!

The difference, indeed, between pure poetry and what is not pure poetry may be strikingly illustrated by placing beside this stanza the very similar lines of the song in *Pippa Passes:*

> The year's at the spring
> And day's at the morn;
> Morning's at seven;
> The hillside's dew-pearled;
> The lark's on the wing;
> The snail's on the thorn:
> God's in his heaven—
> All's right with the world!

Wordsworth invites us to no conclusion, though he undoubtedly wished to make our hearts leap up; Browning's (it would be fairer to say Pippa's) song is, as Mr. Ransom has observed, a piece of transparent homiletics. Wordsworth's kind of pure poetry we may call, without too much wrenching of an accepted term, Imagistic. The heading will cover not only poems like Amy Lowell's, actually labeled Imagistic, but all those poems in which no definite formulation of ideas is made or called for. I would even stretch the term a little and say "no *considerable* formulation of ideas." The stuff of the poem tends to be as nearly pure images as language permits—an important qualification, for language was not developed for the sole purpose of expressing images, and proves highly refractory when so employed.

The other kind of pure poetry is pure, not because it does not require the contemplation of doctrine or ideas, but because the ideas, though present in the mind of the poet, have been squeezed out of the poem and you are expected to supply them yourself as a commentary. Since poetry, to use Mr. Eliot's phrase, resides in the "objective correlative," that is, in the image or symbol of the immediate qualities of experience, all the conventional *structure* of a poem, its connections and transitions, everything that explicitly directs and explains the bits of heightened consciousness, is thought to be mere prose and therefore better omitted. To quote Mr. Eliot again, "The justification of such abbreviation of method is that the sequence of images coincides and concentrates into one *intense* impression."

I think I shall be clearer if, instead of proceeding at once to illustrate from Mr. Eliot, I discuss a very famous impure poem:

That time of year thou mayst in me behold
When yellow leaves, or none, or few, do hang
Upon those boughs which shake against the cold,
Bare ruin'd choirs where late the sweet birds sang.
In me thou see'st the twilight of such day
As after sunset fadeth in the west,
Which by and by black night doth take away,
Death's second self, that seals up all in rest.
In me thou see'st the glowing of such fire
That on the ashes of his youth doth lie,
As the death-bed whereon it must expire,
Consum'd with that which it was nourish'd by.
   This thou perceiv'st, which makes thy love more strong,
   To love that well which thou must leave ere long.

We have here three fine "objective correlatives" (boughs bare of their leaves, clouds darkening in the west, a fire glowing on the ashes just before going out) bound together by a thin thread of "prose" ("thou mayst in me behold," "In me thou see'st," "Death's second self," "of his youth"), and tied firmly with a "prose" application at the end. The contention is that the effect would be more powerful if we could somehow manage to feel the images fully and accurately without having the effect diluted by any words put in to give us a "meaning"—that is, if we could expel all the talk *about* the imaginative realization and have the pure realization itself.

Take now the first, second, and fifth stanzas of Mr. Eliot's *Ash-Wednesday:*

> Because I do not hope to turn again
> Because I do not hope
> Because I do not hope to turn
> Desiring this man's gift and that man's scope
> I no longer strive to strive towards such things
> (Why should the agèd eagle stretch its wings?)
> Why should I mourn
> The vanished power of the usual reign?
>
> Because I do not hope to know again
> The infirm glory of the positive hour
> Because I do not think
> Because I know I shall not know
> The one veritable transitory power
> Because I cannot drink
> There, where trees flower, and springs flow,
>   for there is nothing again
>
> .   .   .   .
>
> Because these wings are no longer wings to fly
> But merely vans to beat the air
> The air which is now thoroughly small and dry

Smaller and dryer than the will
Teach us to care and not to care
Teach us to sit still.

Pray for us sinners now and at the hour of our death
Pray for us now and at the hour of our death.

It would not be honest to say that I "understand" these
stanzas as I do Shakespeare's sonnet. Shakespeare has taken
no chance on my mistaking the general "meaning" of his
images. But one thing is clear: Mr. Eliot wants me to supply
a great deal that is not in the poem. His particular variety
of purity consists in referring to other literary works, a
knowledge of which will indicate his "meaning." First, he
wants me to bring to my reading an intimate knowledge
of the portion of the prophet Joel appointed for the Epistle
on Ash Wednesday, and as the poem goes on, a great deal
more from the Bible and the service books of the Church;
for example, the *Hail Mary* with which my extract ends.
He expects me to recognize the fact that his first line is
a literal translation of the first line of a *ballata* by Guido
Cavalcanti, and that his fourth line is taken, with the
change of one word ("gift" for "art"), from Shakespeare's
twenty-ninth sonnet. I think, though I cannot be sure of
it, that he also wishes me to keep pretty constantly in mind
Wordsworth's *Ode: Intimations of Immortality*, which,
like the poems of Cavalcanti and Shakespeare, is in part
the expression of a mood of despondency, of a wish to return to a more favored state. And it is certain that as a
background to the entire poem—fulfilling much the same
function as that of Frazer's *Golden Bough* and Miss
Weston's *From Ritual to Romance* in *The Waste Land*—he

97

presupposes an acquaintance with *The Dark Night of the Soul*, a devotional work by a sixteenth-century Spanish mystic, St. John of the Cross.

Let me attempt a pure prose paraphrase. The stanzas are an expression of a special kind of spiritual dryness, of that bleakness and depression of soul which St. John calls the dark night of sense and the dark night of spirit. To certain favored souls who have made some progress in the spiritual life, God grants the possibility of the highest of all religious experiences, mystical union with Himself. As a condition of this union, the soul must pass through a period of darkness and deprivation in order to be purged of its pride and self-will. In this state it is purely passive, being incapable of savoring either the pleasures of sense or the joys of the spirit; and although it is actually making progress towards God, it feels only complete wretchedness, and is convinced that the weight of its unhappiness will never be lifted. The poet, who is experiencing this state, is called, with all other men, on the solemn day marking the beginning of Lent, to turn to the Lord, with all his heart, and with fasting, and with weeping, and with mourning— mourning, that is, for the sins of flesh and spirit that alienate men from God. In the state in which he is, the summons seems somewhat ironical, and he meditates on it not without bitterness. The phrase "turn to the Lord" in the Epistle recalls to his mind the *ballata* of Cavalcanti (*Perch' io non spero di tornar giammai*), in which Cavalcanti, writing from exile, says that as he is enfeebled and wretched and has no hope of ever returning to Tuscany, he sends this poem to his lady, to plead for him. The poet thinks, I have no hope of turning again either to God or to the vanities of the flesh. Like Shakespeare in the sonnet, I beweep my outcast state and only feel my impotence as compared with other men. Why should I mourn the sort of sins the Epistle is talking about? Their power is vanished. He does not say, as a true penitent should, that he has deliberately renounced all the vanities of flesh and spirit, but he offers, for whatever it may be worth, the fact that he no longer has them and no longer has even a hope of returning to them. And because he no longer hopes to sin, he prays that God will not judge him too severely; and since he does not ask any more for the blessedness of complete acceptance, he feels that he may ask God to teach him, while he cares for salvation, not to care too much: to teach him to endure his desolation without striving and struggling. A very dull paraphrase this, for by painful effort I have eschewed all figurative language, whereas the original is presented almost entirely without the use of direct statements to be taken in their literal sense. Instead we have unglossed symbols: the agèd eagle, the garden where springs flow, the thin dry air of the desert.

This variety of pure poetry I shall call "Elliptical." Many of our critics call its modern manifestation "Metaphysical," and profess to find its essence in its tendency to use firm and developed images with several points of relevancy, rather than the shifting and dissolving imagery, relevant only here and there, which the Romantics affected. But I need a term that will include other varieties of pure poetry besides the modern, and "elliptical" seems to me to hit the mark. To the ordinary reader the prime characteristic of this kind of poetry is not the nature of its imagery but its obscurity: its urgent suggestion that you add something to the poem without telling you what that something is. "Elliptical" will cover not only poems of Donne and Eliot, but also Collins's *Ode on the Poetical Character*, much of Blake, and some of Browning. The great difference, it seems to me, between obscure poetry of our day and that of the past is that the modern poet goes much farther in employing private experience or ideas than would formerly have been thought legitimate. Milton's *Paradise Lost* is one of the most allusive poems ever written, and to a Hindu who had learned the English language but knew nothing of the Bible or the Greek and Roman classics, would be a desperately obscure poem, but Milton planned to keep the allusions within the range of the cultivated English reader of his day.

Mr. Eliot's pure poetry does not seem much like Amy Lowell's; nor do either of them appear to be talking the same language as the Abbé Bremond, who seriously equates the poetic with the mystic experience, and regards prayer (in a technical, Catholic sense) as its nearest analogue. But all three could stem from, and find a common denominator in Poe. What Poe did, essentially, was to head a revolt against the subjection of poetic speech to the practical sense —to "reason" or "science," to the arrogant tendency of the mind not to linger in a pure realization or enjoyment of experience, but to do something about it—at least to order and file it so that it will be available for action later. Purity in poetry is freedom from explicit message, from annotation or interpretation, from "meaning" in the ordinary sense.

I said at the outset that I should question the desirability of pure poetry, if such an article were found to exist, but of course what I really question is the desirability of setting up an ideal of pure poetry as a critical norm. Wherever pure poetry, either imagistic or elliptical, comes into being as a genuine expression of a sensibility, it is obviously a good thing. In contemporary poetry the pure-poetry dogma serves the same purpose as the "rules" of the seventeenth and eighteenth centuries; however little general validity it may have, it is certainly to some extent a definition of our basis of feeling. But when it is erected into a general critical principle by which the literature of other epochs is to be tested, it collides violently with the doctrine which I am trying to establish.

I wonder if the scientists are not wiser (or, if you prefer, less naïve) than the literary critics? For scientists have a very clear understanding that purity is one thing when you are theorizing and another when you are manufacturing.

Every person with even a smattering of science knows that all the tables of reference for, let us say, freezing points and boiling points are for "pure" substances: pure water, pure ethyl alcohol, pure acetic acid. "Pure" water freezes at zero and boils at 100° centigrade, but all of us who have driven an automobile in the winter know that water with some alcohol in it will boil before the thermometer reaches 100°, and must be cooled below zero before it will freeze. Students even of elementary chemistry know that there are two kinds of chemicals in the laboratory: chemicals which are good enough for most experiments, and others, ordinarily called "chemically pure" ("C.P."), which must be used in qualitative and quantitative analysis. If you used C.P. reagents when the ordinary kind would have done just as well, you were probably lectured by your instructor for your wastefulness or pedantry.

Here is one of those bottles containing a C.P. chemical.[1] It bears the distinctive Merck label which any one at all at home in a laboratory can recognize at a glance. Let us see what it says:

Reagent
SODIUM CARBONATE
ANHYDROUS
Conforms to A.C.S. Specifications

Maximum Impurities

Insoluble matter	0.010%	Aluminum (Al_2O_3) .	0.005 %
Loss on Ignition	1.0 %	Arsenic (As)	0.0001%
Chloride (Cl)	0.003%	Calcium and Magne-	
Sulphur Compounds		sium Precip.	0.010 %
(as SO_4)	0.004%	Iron (Fe)	0.0005%
Nitrogen Compounds		Other Heavy Metals	
(as N)	0.001%	(as Pb)	0.0005%
Phosphate (PO_4)	0.002%	Potassium (K) abt. ...	0.02 %
Silica (SiO_2)	0.005%		

This surely is extraordinary. "Chemically pure" or "C.P." appears to be only vulgar terminology, for the label assures us at great length that the substance is impure. It gives us that assurance in a table that makes it possible for us to compute that if we had 100 kilograms of the substance, the impurities would amount to 1060 grams. Or, in avoirdupois measure, 220 pounds of the substance would contain two and a third pounds of impurities. Even eliminating the water, which constitutes the greater part of the impurity, there would still be left more than two ounces of potassium, calcium, magnesium, insoluble matter, and the rest. Yet this is an excellent C.P. chemical.

[1] These lectures were delivered in a chemical lecture room.

But let us continue our chemical analogy. "Pure water" is a phrase with which we are all familiar. We want "pure" water to drink. The manufacturer of artificial ice wants "pure" water for his process. The physicist wants "pure" water as a standard: many of his scales depend on it. Now "pure" means something different in each of these cases. "Pure" drinking water is water without impurities which are offensive to sight, smell, or taste, or which, though impalpable to the senses, are injurious to health. A "pure" drinking water actually contains dissolved gases, and may show a considerable residue of mineral salts. The dissolved gases and some of the mineral salts, which would be considered immaterial or beneficial in a "pure" drinking water, are the very impurities which a maker of artificial ice must remove, for they cause cloudiness in his product. The physicist wants to remove *all* impurities—dissolved gases and all foreign substances whatsoever. A fish could not live in his "pure" water, and no one would drink it from choice. But of course even he can never bring water to a state of absolute purity.

There is no such thing as a chemically pure substance: none has ever been prepared, none ever can be prepared. "Chemically pure" substances are imaginary or ideal. The term, as a philosopher would say, is merely a "limiting concept." That is, we can, by patient and laborious processes of refining, bring a substance closer and closer to the state of purity, but we can never reach that state. "C.P." merely means that chemicals so designated are pure enough for a particular purpose. You can tell whether that is pure enough for *your* purpose by reading the label.

It is simply not true in practical chemistry that a more

highly refined substance is in all circumstances to be preferred. One of the first marks of a good chemical engineer is his skill in using unrefined chemicals. Refining is expensive, and if the unrefined substance is good enough for practical purposes, it is sheer pedantry to employ the refined. The rule applies to all engineering: be sure that your materials are good enough for the job; never employ unnecessary refinements. May I suggest that those who deal with theory of poetry resemble the theoretical physicists, but that poets should be regarded as engineers?

The doctrine of pure poetry is a necessary part of theory of poetry. No one can define, or attempt to define, poetry without consciously or unconsciously employing the concept. But pure poetry, like a chemically pure substance, is imaginary or ideal. It belongs exclusively to the realm of theory. It is as impossible to write a completely pure poem as it is to produce a completely pure chemical. The real question one should ask in both cases is, "How pure does it need to be?" Poets when they are writing poems and critics when they are criticizing them should take care not to be too much preoccupied with theory. The same wastefulness occurs when you carry a general demand for pure poetry into practical criticism that would occur if you carried a demand for chemically pure substances into engineering. Please understand that I am not attacking good modern poetry because its specifications seem to demand a higher degree of purity than has hitherto been usual. If the answer to the question, "How pure does it need to be?" is "Pretty pure, if the expression of sensibility is to be valid," then we shall not quarrel if the poet hands us Imagistic or Elliptical poetry. We should not ask the poets to be other than themselves. But can we not urge them to *be* themselves, in spite of critical pressure? The definition of the sensibility of an age becomes the vice of that age; and purity in poetry is our vice, as "correctness" in poetry was the vice of the neo-classics. Can we not say to the poets, "We are grateful for your obscure poetry, but please don't think that on our account you have to make it any more obscure than you otherwise would." This is not all joking. I once knew an esteemed minor poetess who admitted that after she had written a poem to her own satisfaction, she rewrote it so as to make it more obscure, obscure poetry being so much more respected. Goethe said of Byron that he produced his poems as women do pretty children: they do not think about it and do not know how it is done. It would not do us any harm to have more poets like Byron.

The great objection to the dogma of pure poetry when it is generally applied is that it forces us to take the position which I have deprecated in the case of Wordsworth: that a very large part of the esteemed poetry of the past is good *in spite of* some serious defect. "Didactic poetry," said Shelley in the preface to *Prometheus Unbound*, "is my abhorrence"; thus perhaps inaugurating one of the most confidently held of our modern poetic principles. But— *The Faerie Queene*, the *Essay on Man*, *The Seasons*, *The Vanity of Human Wishes*, *The Deserted Village*, *The Excursion!* It is true, as I have been at some pains to say, that the aesthetic impulse is not the same thing as the conscious will to instruct. That is theory. But when it comes to actual poems, the impurity of didacticism may be no disadvantage at all. It is as absurd to say that the didactic impulse necessarily withers and destroys all contiguous poetry as it would be to say that the nitrogen in the air renders it unfit for breathing. I have mentioned *The Excursion*, a ticklish case, for that poem was written when the time-honored didactic framework was ceasing to be expressive. Coleridge's disappointment with it warns us that it is not merely shift of sensibility that makes parts of it seem flat and lifeless. But Coleridge's judgment was, after all, only relative: he was comparing the actual poem with the one he expected Wordsworth to write. Any reader who can rid himself of the prejudice which tells him that he must refuse to be pleased when he finds himself being indoctrinated, will find *The Excursion* a noble poem filled with memorable images and as exciting as a novel. I dislike the dogma of pure poetry, because, by making us too exclusively theorists, it robs us of so much pleasure. It produces in us the same frigidity that the dogma of "reason" and the rules induced in earlier generations. I cannot help feeling that our attacks on Romantic poetry will sound in time just like Rymer's assault on Beaumont and Fletcher.

But if poetry does not need to be pure, on what theoretical ground can one find fault with anything in a poem? What right had I to criticize the prosaisms in Wordsworth's *Thorn?* What kind of prosaism is acceptable and what is not?

That appears to me at the moment the hardest question in theory of poetry, and I am not sure that I ought to attempt an answer. But it occurs to me that the element of prose is innocent and even salutary when it appears as— take your choice of three metaphors—a background on which the images are projected, or a frame in which they are shown, or a thread on which they are strung. In short, when it serves a *structural* purpose. Prose in a poem seems offensive to me when (as in that stanza of the *Thorn*) the prosaisms are sharp, obvious, individual, and ranked coordinately with the images.

Poetry should be no purer than the purpose demands. The sensibility of our modern age seems to demand an unusually high degree of purity, and there is nothing more to be said about it. To accuse all our best living poets of being affected and pretentious is too desperate a recourse. But surely a reader whose age is already beginning to qualify him for classification as an old fogey can cast an envious eye at those ages when poetry was robustly and innocently impure, when poetry threw its mantle over all kinds of writing. Without saying that we should try to imitate them, we may, I think, regard as the "greatest" periods of literature those like the Elizabethan and the Romantic, when the poetic spirit was fecund and confident, when poets wrote long poems and many of them, when didactic and satirical and narrative poetry flourished alongside the lyric, which seems to be about the only "kind" now recognized. An age that could produce a Byron, a Wordsworth, and a Walter Scott is not to be held in contempt, but to be envied. Which is only another way of saying that the "great" ages in literature are the impure ones. They are great because they stand a better chance of achieving complexity of value.

VI

EMERGENT IDIOM

On February 1, 1793, the youthful French Republic declared war on England. Five days later Joseph Johnson, a "liberal" publisher of St. Paul's Churchyard, London, announced the simultaneous publication of two thin quarto pamphlets: *An Evening Walk* and *Descriptive Sketches*, poems in the heroic couplet by W. Wordsworth, B.A. of St. John's College, Cambridge. Young Mr. Wordsworth, who displayed his degree so prominently on his title pages, had no particular reason to be proud of it. He had shown more interest in learning Italian than in mastering the mathematical subjects required for academic preferment, and in the summer vacation of 1790, when he should have been grinding for his degree, had gone off on a walking-tour in the Alps. He had been graduated in January, 1791, without honors and apparently without any intention of betaking himself to a profession. In the autumn of that year he went back to France, ostensibly for the purpose of acquiring the French language. France was then passing through the most momentous portion of the Revolution. When young Mr. Wordsworth returned at the end of 1792, he was thoroughly imbued with republican zeal and had acquired an illegitimate daughter. He hastened to add to his productions (as Boswell said in similar circumstances) by publishing these two poems: the first begun in a different form at Hawkshead in the spring of 1787, while he was still a schoolboy, and added to during his college vacations of 1788 and 1789, the other commemorating his walking-tour of 1790. The first, I think, was completely reshaped and rewritten on the banks of the Loire in 1792, and the second entirely composed at that time. The poems must have been put to press immediately upon his arrival. He still showed a discouraging reluctance to provide himself with a means of livelihood.

The fact was that young Mr. Wordsworth knew that he was a poet, planned to be a great poet, and intended to allow nothing to interfere with his calling. In that long vacation of 1788 at Hawkshead, on coming home through the fields after a dance that had lasted all night, there had come to him one of those sublime and crucial moments which he afterwards called "spots of time"; moments which came to him not too frequently but authentically; moments when he could see into the life of things.

> Magnificent
> The morning was, in memorable pomp,
> More glorious than I ever had beheld.
> The Sea was laughing at a distance; all
> The solid Mountains were as bright as clouds,
> Grain-tinctured, drench'd in empyrean light;
> And in the meadows and the lower grounds,
> Was all the sweetness of a common dawn,
> Dews, vapours, and the melody of birds,
> And Labourers going forth into the fields.

—Ah! need I say, dear Friend, that to the brim
My heart was full; I made no vows, but vows
Were then made for me; bond unknown to me
Was given, that I should be, else sinning greatly,
A dedicated Spirit.

This great experience came a few months after his
eighteenth birthday, and coincides with the writing of part
of *The Vale of Esthwaite*, which was to be worked over
into *An Evening Walk*. His great poetical autobiography,
The Prelude, gives us a delightfully intimate picture of the
poet (remember, not a craggy-faced old man with woolly
side whiskers but a homely boy of eighteen with stringy
dark hair, a big nose, and flashing eyes) at work on his
poem. He walked out, day after day, with a dog, a rough-
haired terrier, composing orally as he walked, a lifelong
practice with him. The dog, though puzzled and wearied
by his dilatory progress and strange haltings, remained
loyally with him to protect him from human beings who
might be less understanding. As the boy Wordsworth
sauntered along the road muttering to himself, the dog
would run on ahead and see if any one was coming; if he
spied a passenger, he would run back to warn his master
and give him time to compose himself. And, says Wordsworth,

A hundred times when, in these wanderings,
I have been busy with the toil of verse,
Great pains and little progress, and at once
Some fair enchanting image in my mind
Rose up, full-form'd, like Venus from the sea,
Have I sprung forth towards him, and let loose
My hand upon his back with stormy joy,
Caressing him again, and yet again.

This introduction may seem tediously detailed, but it is my purpose to analyze those fair enchanting images. And before we begin, it is important for us to recall the fact that *An Evening Walk* was in its inspiration and inception a boy's poem. Perhaps no piece that Wordsworth ever wrote seemed to him at the time of composition quite so miraculous. I have chosen it, not because it is a perfect composition—it is far from being that—but because, by enabling us to see a powerful and original genius grappling with the problem of poetic idiom, it will enable us to illustrate the painfully abstract matter of the earlier lectures. And it will also enable us to extend our conclusions concerning the general desirability of purity in poetry.

Wordsworth, as we have seen, began the piece in 1787, but he did not publish it until 1793. We have not previously had any knowledge of the nature of the earlier drafts. The publication last month (February, 1941) of the first volume of Professor de Selincourt's new critical edition of the *Poetical Works*—the most exciting event in Wordsworth studies since the same editor's critical edition of the texts of *The Prelude* in 1926—provides us with a gratifying amount of evidence, but the bearing of it is not perfectly clear. No complete manuscript anterior to publication has been found, but Mr. de Selincourt has recovered a fragmentary notebook preserving earlier drafts of about half the poem. These he thinks "probably" of the Cambridge period, that is, either actual first drafts or revisions made very soon after the original composition. If so, the poem was little changed before publication. But my own conclusion is that the poem written in 1788 and 1789 was the octosyllabic *Vale of Esthwaite*, now first published in a fragmentary state by Mr. de Selincourt, and that the drafts in the notebook are a reworking of portions of this, a task undertaken by Wordsworth in France in 1792, when we know he wrote the *Descriptive Sketches*. One would like to be sure, but for our purpose it does not much matter whether the poem as printed represents Wordsworth at eighteen or at twenty-two. In either case it will definitely rank as juvenilia in the Wordsworth canon.

Let us suppose that we have never seen *An Evening Walk*, and are going to read it just as though we now had Wordsworth's quarto in our hands and nothing else. We shall want notes—indeed a shelf full of books—later, but our first reading had better be unimpeded and unaided.

It will take us a considerable time to get through the 446 lines. The author, after the comfortable eighteenth-century fashion, has provided an "Argument," from which we learn that the general framework of the poem is per-ambulatory and horological. We are in the Lake Country: the time is noon of a hot summer day. We take a walk, and, as the afternoon wears on, we view a cascade, notice a peculiar effect of slanting light across the face of a preci-pice, visit a mountain farm and observe a cock of brilliant plumage, and watch from a distance the activity of a stone quarry. It is now sunset. We recall some of the local super-stitions connected with sunset. As evening falls, we walk beside the lake watching two handsome swans with their young: the solicitation of the mother swan for her cygnets and their serene well-being sets us to pondering on the dismal fate of some poor beggar woman with *her* two babes, a soldier's widow, perhaps, whose husband lies

Asleep on Bunker's charnel hill afar.

We picture her toiling hopelessly up the mountain road through the heat; then our pitying fancy goes on and imagines her refused shelter in the winter, and perishing with her children in a storm. As the light fails, we distinguish sounds, unnoticed before. We watch the last gleams of light in the west and on the lake, now silvered with moonlight where the breezes ruffle the water. Night falls, the moon rises higher. Night sounds are heard. The poem ends.

Even with the help of the argument, it is still very hard going. We shall find that we have attempted few poems in which it was so hard to keep the mind in the state of alertness required to hold together what we were reading. If we lose our place, we might as well go back to the beginning and start over. This, we decide, is partly due to the syntax, which is harsh and elliptical to a degree unusual in the heroic couplet. In the third line, instead of (as one would expect)

Where hoary Derwent takes his wizard course,

we actually find

His wizard course where hoary Derwent takes,

and such inversions are extremely common throughout the poem. In the seventeenth line we are puzzled to find "gaze" used in the sense of "gaze at." M. Legouis, we shall discover later, has exhaustively catalogued all these syntactical and grammatical distortions: I can only hint at them. Another source of obscurity is the young poet's passion for personifying everything. In the eight lines beginning with the twenty-eighth, Life rears up the sun; Transport kisses away a tear; Mirth, linked with the poet, courses the plain; Content forsakes her seat; Impatience, panting upward, shows the mountain summits. Farther on, Quiet leads the poet up the brook, and obsequious Grace pursues the swan. They inverted and personified in Pope's time, but nothing like this. Indeed, we come to see that one of the chief causes of the difficulty of the poem is that the author wants to present everything through an image. The great bulk of the lines consists of detailed bits of natural description: visual or auditory images, and the very language in which these images is imbedded is tortured into images too. And some lines are hopelessly obscure just from a reluctance to explain a private image. For example, has anybody *ever* understood the second line in the following? (Wordsworth is mentioning sights particularly moving to him because of their evocations of boyhood memories:)

> A form discover'd at the well-known seat,
> A spot, that angles at the riv'let's feet,
> The cot the ray of morning trav'ling nigh
> And sail that glides the well-known alders by.

"A spot that angles at the rivulet's feet" seems queer, but no queerer than other things in this poem. I have always interpreted it, "A triangular spot of land, a sort of delta, where the rivulet divides into two branches as it enters the lake." Nothing of the sort. The variants now published by Mr. de Selincourt show that "a spot" means "a schoolboy," and "angling" means "fishing": "A schoolboy fishing at the mouth of the brook." Seen from a great distance the boy no doubt was a "spot," or, as I should probably say, a "speck," but how could Wordsworth suppose that any one else could interpret correctly a line with two such ambiguous words in it as *spot* and *angles?* The *foot* of a rivulet is surely unusual, though not too harsh, for this rivulet no doubt descended to the lake in a sharp incline, and we are accustomed to speaking of the foot of the stairs or the foot of a ladder. But unless we are to read *rivulets'* (and not only the pointing of the text of 1793 but also that of the manuscript revision of 1794 is against it), *feet* is surely forced by the rhyme.

In spite of the slow going, and in spite of the generalized diction, which for some reason or other seems particularly offensive in this poem, we should all feel that the poem contained an extraordinary number of clearly perceived and often sharply expressed images—perhaps more than any other poem of equal length we have ever read. Here is a fair sample, not perhaps the most brilliant in the poem, but easier to follow without book than most:

> When, in the south, the wan noon, brooding still,
> Breath'd a pale steam around the glaring hill,
> And shades of deep-embattl'd clouds were seen
> Spotting the northern cliffs with lights between;
> Gazing the tempting shades to them deny'd,
> When stood the shorten'd herds amid the tide,
> Where, from the barren wall's unshelter'd end,
> Long rails into the shallow lake extend;
> When schoolboys stretch'd their length upon the green;
> And round the humming elm, a glimmering scene,
> In the brown park, in flocks, the troubl'd deer
> Shook the still-twinkling tail and glancing ear;
> When horses in the wall-girt intake stood,
> Unshaded, eying far below the flood,
> Crouded behind the swain, in mute distress,
> With forward neck the closing gate to press;
> And long, with wistful gaze, his walk survey'd,
> Till dipp'd his pathway in the river shade . . .

I cannot vouch for the deer, but the cows and horses are caught to the life.

In view of the sharpness and accuracy of the images, we shall probably wonder why we cannot remember the poem better. For it is surely one of the least *memorable* poems ever written. Only two bits are likely to remain with us: the swans and the female vagrant. The closed couplet, we shall probably decide, has something to do with the lack of unity: it slits the pictures up into strips. And also we shall probably agree that there are too many images, and that we don't know in the final reckoning what they all amount to.

A review of contemporary criticism assures us that we have not missed much in the poem because of the lapse of time. Wordsworth, though he was always proud of the fact that there was not an image in it that he had not himself observed, in later years had no high opinion of the piece. In 1801 he called it a "juvenile production, inflated and obscure," though he insisted that it possessed "many new images and vigorous lines." He printed only extracts from it in his first collected edition (1815), and before reprinting it as a whole in 1820 revised it so drastically as to make it almost a new poem. Dorothy Wordsworth's opinion coincided with her brother's. Coleridge, in his volume of 1796, paid tribute to "Mr. Wordsworth, a Poet whose versification is occasionally harsh and his diction too frequently obscure; but whom [he goes on] I deem unrivalled among the writers of the present day in manly sentiment, novel imagery, and vivid colouring." ("Manly sentiment" surely must refer to the companion poem, *Descriptive*

Sketches, for *An Evening Walk* contains hardly anything to justify such language.) But the best summary ever made of the virtues and defects of the poem occurs in the fourth chapter of the *Biographia Literaria:*

"During the last year of my residence at Cambridge, I became acquainted with Mr. Wordsworth's first publication [he says, *Descriptive Sketches*, but everything I am extracting will apply equally well to our poem]; and seldom, if ever, was the emergence of an original poetic genius above the literary horizon more evidently announced. In the form, style, and manner of the whole poem, and in the structure of the particular lines and periods, there is an harshness and acerbity connected and combined with words and images all a-glow, which might recall those products of the vegetable world, where gorgeous blossoms rise out of the hard and thorny rind and shell, within which the rich fruit was elaborating. [What plant did Coleridge have in mind? Are there any plants in which flowers grow out of fruits? Or are the 'gorgeous blossoms' parasitic?] The language was not only peculiar and strong, but at times knotty and contorted, as by its own impatient strength; while the novelty and struggling crowd of images, acting in conjunction with the difficulties of the style, demanded always a greater closeness of attention than poetry (at all events, than descriptive poetry) has a right to claim."

He makes the other defects of the poem clearer by comparing it with Wordsworth's next extended effort, *Salisbury Plain*, the original of *Guilt and Sorrow:*

"There was here [in *Salisbury Plain*] no mark of strained thought, or forced diction, no crowd or turbulence of imagery; and, as the poet hath himself well described in his lines 'on re-visiting the Wye,' manly reflection and human associations had given both variety and an additional interest to natural objects, which in the passion and appetite of the first love they had seemed to him neither to need or permit. The occasional obscurities, which had risen from an imperfect controul over the resources of his native language, had almost wholly disappeared, together with that worse defect of arbitrary and illogical phrases, at once hackneyed and fantastic, which hold so distinguished a place in the *technique* of ordinary poetry, and will more or less alloy the earlier poems of the truest genius, unless the attention has been specifically directed to their worthlessness and incongruity."

In short, in *An Evening Walk* Wordsworth had not yet struck out the idiom proper to the new sensibility though he was struggling to do so; and secondly, he had made the mistake of writing too pure a poem.

"Nature"—that is, landscape, with or without other human beings than the poet in it—is not a fixed, objective thing of determinate qualities which poets from the beginning of time have been trying to paint in words. The only persons to whom Nature presents itself in those terms are the natural scientists. A mountain is granite or it is basalt; a loon builds a nest or it does not; a rhododendron will die if its roots touch chalk, and no doubt about it. But the "description of Nature" which appears in poems, though it may occasionally make a parade of botanical or geological knowledge, really has nothing whatever to do with that sort of record. Poetry is a description of mental states; it uses natural objects only as they are expressive of those states.

Here is a daffodil, a good normal specimen of *Narcissus pseudonarcissus*. To a botanist there is only one possible way to describe it. It has so many sepals, so many petals, stamens so-and-so, pistil so-and-so—bulb, leaves, approximate height, distribution, etc., etc. But Herrick could look at a daffodil and see it as an emblem of mortality:

> When a Daffadill I see,
> Hanging down his head t'wards me;
> Guess I may, what I must be.
> First, I shall decline my head;
> Secondly, I shall be dead;
> Lastly, safely buryed.

To Wordsworth daffodils were an objective correlative, not to man's decline and death, but to joy.

Successful descriptive poetry does not attempt, in the scientific manner, to catalogue objects precisely. It becomes successful when it realizes that its real subject matter is not lakes or mountains, rivulets or precipices, birds or flowers, but man's inner life, the motions and changes of which, in some mysterious fashion, may be symbolized by the elements of landscape. And perhaps it does not become successful even then. It must realize the precise quality of this mental life which is its subject matter and not only select its symbols but direct them. Unsuccessful descriptive poetry either errs by trying to depict everything with detail enough to make identification possible in the scientist's sense, or it suppresses to the point of obscurity the passages of "reflection and human associations." It presents pseudo-science or poetry that is overly pure.

Let us shift the scene.

In the year 1713, in this very month of March, young Mr. Pope, a crooked clever Papist lad who had already published his *Pastorals*, the *Essay on Criticism*, and the first version of *The Rape of the Lock*, brought out his *Windsor Forest*, a locodescriptive poem in heroic couplets, running to some 430 lines—approximately the same length as *An Evening Walk*. In its original form it had been composed at a very early age. Pope said at sixteen, and the critics have perhaps shown themselves too suspicious in accusing him of always antedating his juvenile works so as to emphasize his precocity. It was certainly in existence in some form or other in 1707, when Pope was nineteen. But in the absence of manuscript proof, a poem sent by him to the printer at the same time as *The Rape of the Lock* can hardly be considered a really juvenile performance. The concluding portion of 150 lines, indeed, was quite new, having been written to celebrate the Peace of Utrecht, which had not yet been ratified, but was known to be certain of ratification.

Let us now approach this poem as we did Wordsworth's.

We shall find few obstacles so far as style is concerned. Pope's passion for conciseness sometimes results in obscure lines, but they are only relatively obscure, little eddies in a stream that is remarkably smooth and rapid. We can probably get through his poem in a fifth of the time we had to spend on Wordsworth's. If anything, we feel, we should be grateful (to change the figure to Coleridge's) for a little more knottiness in the texture. There are quantities of pagan deities and mythology; there is the usual wealth of antithesis and point; and there is a great deal of elegance and periphrasis. Farmers are industrious swains, young sportsmen are vigorous swains, partridges are betrayed to the spaniel by the tainted gales, a gun is a tube, bird-shot are leaden death, and fish are the scaly breed. No reader of the present day is likely to experience tremors down the spine at more than bits here and there. He will find some lines that, taken by themselves, give him, without any sense of quaintness, the intrinsic realization of poetic feeling that we look for in poetry. I should instance

> And in the new-shorn field the partridge feeds,

and

> When frosts have whitened all the naked groves,

and

> His shadow lengthened by the setting sun.

There are other passages which strike us as being quaint but very lovely:

> There, interspersed in lawns and opening glades,
> Thin trees arise that shun each other's shades.
> Here in full light the russet plains extend:
> There wrapt in clouds the blueish hills ascend.
> Even the wild heath displays her purple dyes,
> And 'midst the desert fruitful fields arise,
> That crowned with tufted trees and springing corn,
> Like verdant isles the sable waste adorn.

Or this:

> The levelled towns with weeds lie covered o'er;
> The hollow winds through naked temples roar;
> Round broken columns clasping ivy twined;
> O'er heaps of ruin stalked the stately hind;
> The fox obscene to gaping tombs retires,
> And savage howlings fill the sacred quires.

Some of the bits are more gorgeous. I shall not repeat the famous passage on the whirring pheasant as being too familiar, but venture to offer as a substitute the following aquarium piece:

> Our plenteous streams a various race supply,
> The bright-eyed perch with fins of Tyrian dye,
> The silver eel, in shining volumes rolled,
> The yellow carp, in scales bedropped with gold,
> Swift trouts, diversified with crimson stains,
> And pikes, the tyrants of the watery plains.

And finally, my favorite, though Joseph Warton thought the lines "puerile and redundant":

> Oft in her [the Loddon's] glass the musing shepherd spies
> The headlong mountains and the downward skies,
> The watery landscape of the pendent woods,
> And absent trees that tremble in the floods;
> In the clear azure gleam the flocks are seen,
> And floating forests paint the waves with green,
> Through the fair scene roll slow the ling'ring streams,
> Then foaming pour along, and rush into the Thames.

But, take it all in all, there seems to be an intolerable deal of reflection for a pennyworth of description. We should be glad to exchange Sir William Trumbull and

Lord Granville and even Queen Anne for some more pheasants. It would not have occurred to us that a descriptive poem on Windsor Forest had much to do with the Peace of Utrecht, and even after we have seen how Pope manages it (the Thames runs through Windsor Forest—Father Thames rises, bows in the direction of Windsor Castle, and announces that the Peace will bring boundless commerce into his stream), we are not sure that it should have been managed. But unquestionably the extended images of the poem are very memorable and pleasant.

When in poetry we see a thing, which, though strange, seems to be done according to a system, it is a warning to us that we had better make sure that we understand the system. Suppose we analyze the structure of *Windsor Forest*. Wordsworth's thread of connection, you will remember, is no more than what he calls it: a walk and the passage of the hours. Pope's proves to be quite different. In his first couplet he announces his subject matter, which is to be Windsor's forest and its green retreats, the abodes alike of the monarch and the muses. The forest and green retreats get one line, and the monarch and muses one. It is clear, then, that Pope has not deceived us, for he promised us at the outset description and something else, presumably politics and literature. Then come the conventional invocation of the nymphs and naiads, and a reference to Granville, who has commanded the poem. We are under way.

The groves of Eden, though long vanished, says Pope, live in Milton's song; if I had his ability, these groves should have equal fame. *Paradise Lost* naturally suggests creation: here in Windsor Forest the various kinds of landscape seem to strive again as on the day when God composed them, not mixed without plan, as in chaos, but harmoniously confused, a type of the world. Then follows the first painting which I have transcribed. A painting I call it, for it is that: very general and unparticularized in detail, leaving a great deal of freedom to the reader, who perhaps has not seen the country around Windsor, to make up a visual image from his own experience. But the poet gives us only ten descriptive lines, and those are broken by a smart simile. Then, from "springing corn" his mind turns to the products of England generally. India may boast her exotic plants that weep amber and balm; what of it? From the oaks of Windsor Forest are made the ships that bear those precious cargoes to us, and establish our rule over India. We have already, within thirty-two lines, touched on Windsor's green retreats and the muses, and have now prepared an opening for the monarch. This prospect shows all the blessings of the gods: flocks, fruits, flowers, grain. Peace and plenty proclaim the reign of a Stuart—Queen Anne.

It has not always been so. In ages past the land was a desert, a royal forest tyrannically set aside by the Conqueror. Fields were snatched from their owners, towns were leveled. Then follows the second of my transcriptions, the picture of the broken columns and the obscene fox—a very pretty fancy piece. It has, of course, little or no historical truth, but it visualizes readily and effectively. This gives our poet his first opportunity for pointed morality. William, who devoted this huge region to beasts, was himself denied a grave, and his first and second sons met violent deaths in the New Forest. Succeeding monarchs were more benevolent and allowed the cottages, the flocks, and the grain to creep back. Liberty reared her cheerful head again.

Liberty suggests sports—at least suggests them enough so that a glance at the sports of the Forest will not seem incongruous. We see the vigorous swains go out with their dogs, partridge netting, pheasant shooting, coursing hares. Or we watch the fowler leveling his tube at doves, woodcock, lapwings, larks. Or we watch the patient fisher hoping the scaly breed. Or we see the youth hunting the fleet hart with the opening hound. Interspersed are a good number of bright descriptive lines and two set pieces: the murdered pheasant and the lines depicting the fish. Hunting furnishes a transition to Diana, Diana an opportunity for another compliment to Queen Anne. While we are well embarked on mythology, let us have a digression: the metamorphosis, in the best Ovidian manner, of Lodona, a nymph of Diana's train, pursued and ravished by Pan and at her own request turned into a stream. Then another picture, the last of the passages I read to you.

This takes us nearly to the end of the earlier portion of the poem, and will do as a sample of the whole. It cannot escape our notice that Pope, however haphazard he may seem in his introduction of pictures, is really managing them very artificially. It is clear that, though he can turn them off at will, he does not want too many of them. When we stop to consider, we see that a relatively small part of *Windsor Forest* is descriptive in the sense of evoking pictures. The pictures are hung on a spacious background of history and men in action. Is it possible that the relative frigidity of the poem in our experience is due to the fact that because of a shift of sensibility, we do not naturally find landscape expressive any more of history and human pursuits? That since Wordsworth's time, and largely through Wordsworth's efforts, landscape has become expressive in a quite different way?

We had better now seek some help from the early critics. The task, we shall find, is complicated by the fact that all the editors of Pope who have written extensively on *Windsor Forest* (Warton, Bowles, and Elwin) have been Romantics. Warton and Bowles, indeed, were poets, and both did significant service in the formulation of the new aesthetic creed. The only early critic of eminence from whom we can get a genuinely neo-classical report appears to be Dr. Johnson. Warton and Bowles naturally complain of the generalized character of the description, which Bowles indeed attributes to Pope's physical infirmities. Johnson, as naturally, assumes that description *should* be handled in that way. But all three have no doubt that Pope's framework is admirable.

"The design of *Windsor Forest*," says Johnson, "is evidently derived from *Cooper's Hill*, with some attention to Waller's poem on *The Park;* but Pope cannot be denied to excel his masters in variety and elegance, and the art of interchanging description, narrative, and morality." Descriptive poems, he goes on to say, generally lack a regular subordination of parts, because the order in which the scenes is shown is arbitrary, and "more is not to be expected from the last part than from the first. The attention, therefore, which cannot be detained by suspense, must be excited by diversity, such as his poem offers to its reader." If anything, he thought Pope had been too strenuous in providing diversity. Father Thames and the transformation of Lodona might well have been spared. "The story of *Lodona* is told with sweetness; but a new metamorphosis is a ready and puerile expedient; nothing is easier than to tell how a flower was once a blooming virgin, or a rock an obdurate tyrant." As to Lodona, Bowles upholds Johnson; Warton sides with Pope.

Our conclusion, I think, would be that although *Windsor Forest* is not to our sensibility a highly exciting poem, and not to be ranked among Pope's best, it is a successful and very accomplished work of art. Pope has a verse form and a diction perfectly expressive of his subject matter. Nature, for him, expresses civilization and human advance through the centuries. He generalizes his description, not because he was deficient in minute observation (he may have been, but it is not to the point); he does it because he feels general descriptions to be more poetical. He does not express *himself:* he limits himself throughout to reflections that would be proper for anybody. His verse form, with its polish, its balance, its elegance, is the consummate verbal construction for such material. He knows (I think) that his poem will make its effect by its pictures, but if they are to succeed, he must not crowd them. He therefore frames them well and gives them plenty of wall space. That metaphor, in fact, just about hits the level of the poem. Pope never considered it an attempt at the nobler kind of poetry, and could later smile indulgently at it as a piece in which pure description held the place of sense. It aims principally at being decorative, but decorative in the gracious Augustan style. His pictures are like those cool, high-finished paintings of fruits and flowers that one used to admire in the Wallace Collection, hung properly on the walls of a fine room in a house like Prior Park.

Notice that the relative failure of Wordsworth's poem was not due primarily to youth or inexperience. Pope at twenty-five was no doubt a more experienced poet than Wordsworth at twenty-three, but that is not the main thing. Pope had a developed and successful idiom ready to his hand. He could lisp in numbers, for Dryden had provided the numbers. His verse form was clear to him, his subject matter was clear to him. Wordsworth had to fumble for both.

Why Wordsworth wrote his poem in the heroic coup-let at all is something of a mystery. He had not been using it extensively before, and he used it little after. The ju-venilia which Mr. de Selincourt prints contain only one extended piece in that form: the *Lines Written as a School Exercise at Hawkshead*, Wordsworth's first com-position in verse, written when he was fourteen years old. The couplets are musical, clear, and competent, not in the least like those of *An Evening Walk*. And the reason is obvious: he is imitating Pope, even to subject matter. In the days before his own sensibility had defined itself, he too could lisp in Popean numbers. The *School Exercise* was written to order; the other juvenile poems were writ-ten later to please himself. As one would expect, they show strongly the influence of Spenser, Milton (the minor poems), the Wartons, Collins, and Chatterton. There is one bit of translation from Vergil in heroic couplets (no doubt the authority of Dryden was irresistible), but the other pieces are in lyric measures, pseudo-Spenserian stanzas, or octosyllabics. The octosyllabics greatly predominate; indeed considerable portions of *An Evening Walk*, if my conjectures are correct, were originally composed in that meter. It may be that when he passed the stage of experiments and began to face the practical problem of publication, he turned to the heroic couplet, partly as being the form most commonly employed in English descriptive poetry of the eighteenth century, and partly because it was affected by the most popular poet of the day—Erasmus Darwin. But I think an even more potent influence was the alexandrines of the French pastoral poets Delille, Rosset, Roucher, and Saint-Lambert, in whose works he was immersed at the time. It was probably Darwin's example that betrayed him into such a glare of images and such intemperance of personification. But he did not get his obscure and contorted syntax from Darwin, who is remarkably flowing and easy. M. Legouis suggests that here he was turning to the poets whom he really loved: Spenser, Milton, Thomson, Gray, and Collins. That is, he was trying, in a curiously roundabout fashion, to romanticize his medium. But the closed couplet thwarts him. Its balance and antithesis fight with his subject matter. Its elegant generalized diction sorts incongruously with the occasional use of local and dialect terms (*sugh, ghyll, intake*) to which his sounder instinct directs him.

And he does not yet know what his subject matter really is—what it is that nature is expressive of for him. A good part of *An Evening Walk* springs from no more profound poetic impulse than to meditate on the theme, "How dear to my heart are the scenes of my childhood." He likes to dwell lovingly on every detail of the landscape because by so doing he can momentarily pull himself together. There is the possibility of poetry in this; in the mature Wordsworth it will emerge as natural piety binding his days each to each. But the mature Wordsworth does not make catalogues. It might even be said without too violent paradox that the mature Wordsworth does not write descriptive poetry. Here, to an excessive degree, the colors and the forms have nothing beneath them. They seemed to the young Wordsworth to have

> no need of a remoter charm,
> By thought supplied, nor any interest
> Unborrowed from the eye.

Consequently he insists too much on private experience, on particular, unique detail. He gives us a whole wall full of unframed pictures. He has written too pure a poem.

Even so, *An Evening Walk* might have been better if it were nothing but a piece of pure poetry of the imagistic sort. The trouble is that it does have a framework—a vague and ineffective affair that does not seem to support anything. Some deep impulse is troubling the images and preventing them from uniting into the thin but continuous surface that imagistic poetry demands. Wordsworth at times feels an urgency in the objects of nature that goes far beyond anything demanded by the impulse to autobiography, an urgency that the conventional reflective framework of descriptive poetry will not provide sanctions for. He cannot yet define that urgency to himself. He knows, as Coleridge said later, that the piece needs "manly reflection and human associations to give variety and an additional interest to its natural objects," but the proper kind of reflection eludes him. The best he can do is to make a few cursory and half-hearted turns on the consecrated formulas, and to insert the strongly humanitarian episode of the female vagrant.

At the beginning of 1794 Wordsworth was reunited with Dorothy after long and unhappy years of separation. Settled temporarily in Windy Brow, a farmhouse near Keswick, and living on milk and potatoes because of the slenderness of their combined purses, he came back to *An Evening Walk* and made a further attempt to put the piece right. The many lines which he wrote then were never published in their entirety until Mr. de Selincourt's edition gave them to the world. They make an absorbing study. Wordsworth is still trying to get at the deeper thought that underlies his images. He adds many more fine descriptive details, but in general his additions consist of efforts to moralize his song. There is a reflection on death suggested by the churchyard at Grasmere; there is a reflection on the illimitable powers of Science; there is a humanitarian passage directed against cockfighting; there is a pathetic episode of a maiden whose grief leads her at night to the spot in the quarry where her lover was killed; there is a long reflection (very different from Walter Scott!) on the days of the Border Warfare. But finally he abandoned the revision. I suppose he had come to realize that he could never remold the poem. It was something he had outlived; and he could spend his time more profitably on his *Salisbury Plain*, a long humanitarian narrative in Spenserian stanzas which gave him an opportunity to express something that seemed to him at the moment more urgent than natural beauties: his hatred of war and penal institutions and his faith in the revolutionary power of Reason. He was right: the battle that he had to fight and win was a moral and religious battle. That deep urgency which he felt in the images of nature demanded nothing less than moral and religious sanctions. He has told in *The Prelude* of the bitterness of that struggle: of his disillusionment with his own country, of his disillusionment with France and the Revolution, of his revulsion from the icy rationalism of Godwin's *Political Justice*. But Dorothy was at his side to give him eyes and ears, and later the better trained Coleridge helped him to formulate his thought. The religion of Nature which he attained to has been variously called Hartleian and Neo-Platonic, Christian and pantheistic, profound and superficial; worst of all, superfluous. Its orthodoxy and philosophical consistency, though legitimate subjects for discussion, do not concern me here, but the question whether or not it was superfluous does. To my mind, it is so far from being superfluous that if it were removed from Wordsworth in the interest of pure poetry, there would be no Wordsworth left. The moment he had it, everything was clear. He had his subject matter and he had his idiom—not anything so narrow as the ability to write gracefully in a single verse form, but a style capable of informing many verse forms with a new meaning and power. It came to him, as a muscular skill comes after long and painful practice, not gradually but all at once.

Everything before *Lines Left upon a Seat in a Yew-Tree*, which he completed in 1797, is clearly juvenilia; everything after that is as clearly the mature Wordsworth. Henceforth there was to be no fumbling, and little real progress in poetic skill. He was ready to strike, firmly and confidently, the note that was to dominate English poetry for the next hundred years:

> Five years have past; five summers, with the length
> Of five long winters! and again I hear
> These waters, rolling from their mountain-springs
> With a soft inland murmur.—Once again
> Do I behold these steep and lofty cliffs,
> That on a wild secluded scene impress
> Thoughts of more deep seclusion; and connect
> The landscape with the quiet of the sky. . . .
>   For I have learned
> To look on nature, not as in the hour
> Of thoughtless youth; but hearing oftentimes
> The still, sad music of humanity,
> Nor harsh nor grating, though of ample power
> To chasten and subdue. And I have felt
> A presence that disturbs me with the joy
> Of elevated thoughts; a sense sublime
> Of something far more deeply interfused,
> Whose dwelling is the light of setting suns,
> And the round ocean and the living air,
> And the blue sky, and in the mind of man:
> A motion and a spirit, that impels
> All thinking things, all objects of all thought,
> And rolls through all things.[1]

[1] This was the end of the Messenger series as published in 1941

VII

AN ALTERNATIVE BEGINNING
AND A SUMMARY

Since the publication of *The Idiom of Poetry* I have come to think that it might have been better for the argument if I had eschewed references to physics and chemistry and had laid a different ground of scientific reference. The literary mind, as Max Eastman now wryly admits, cannot be persuaded by any argument based on natural science, for it simply runs away from it. Somewhere early in the modern educational process the majority of the people who later become critics and teachers of literature appear to decide not merely that they are not interested in science but that any genuine knowledge of its philosophy is in bad taste. This early division into those who follow "science" and those who devote themselves to the "humanities" is often in my opinion not the reflection of genuine aptitudes but is rather due to social pressure. There is at least an even chance that the man who leads his class in Yale College will be a graduate of a private preparatory school, but the man who wins the highest honors in the Scientific or Engineering School almost invariably comes to Yale from a public high school. It would be interesting to make a survey of the graduates of the most famous preparatory schools of the East and see what proportion of them become scientists and engineers. It is my impression that the number is much too small to be accounted for in terms of natural aptitude. These schools have excellent scientific departments and some study of science is usually required, but boys find that it is not the thing for a gentleman really to understand and like science. Consequently, no matter how many science requirements may be inserted in college programs, very little is accomplished, for the literary mind has already been established, and at the core of the literary mind is a calm and unshakable conviction that science is "vocational" and deals with gadgets, and that a man who wants a liberal education had better not soil his hands with it.

It is too late now to rewrite the whole series of lectures, but in this essay I shall try to sketch an approach which the reader with the literary mind may find more palatable. I shall lay a ground of scientific reference, but I shall eschew the grubby and "vocational" sciences of physics and chemistry in favor of the elegant and bookish science of linguistics, a science in which the literary mind is almost invariably interested, though I regret to say that as a general thing its knowledge is somewhat superstitious. The main argument of relativism can be based equally well on this material; indeed, linguistic material seems more obviously continuous with the matter of literary criticism than anything that can be drawn from physics.

There exist in the world today two general attitudes towards correctness in language. The first of these may be called the conventional or purist attitude. According to this attitude, with which we have all been familiar since we first went to school, there is a correctness in speaking and writing English similar to that which obtains in arithmetic or algebra. This correctness is held to be absolute and permanent, and is defined by a series of rules. There is, for example, a rule that the subject of a verb must be in the nominative case and another that the object of a verb must be in the objective case; there is furthermore a paradigm which states that the nominative of the pronoun of the first person is always "I" and the objective always "me." If the question is asked, "Is it correct to say, 'It is me'?" the answer is immediately and confidently returned in the negative. "It is me" is incorrect because the predicate pronoun is not in the construction of direct or indirect object and therefore cannot be objective. The only nominative form being "I," only "It is I" can be admitted to be correct. Or, to take another example somewhat less hackneyed, the only correct form for the interrogative or relative pronoun in object relation is "whom": "Whom did you see?" Or again, the correct form is not the "Drive slow" which we are accustomed to see on signs, but "Drive slowly," since the proper ending of an adverb is -ly. To summarize, language, by its very nature has a form of correctness from which actual speech deviates. This form is defined by rules that are static and absolute.

I suppose when we are young none of us thinks of questioning this position much, nor is it desirable that we should. While we are mastering the complexities of speech, it is well that we should passively accept the dogma that our way of speaking and writing, like every-thing else about us, is "incorrect," and we should expect to. be referred to a standard or authority. But we must consider the dogma very unsatisfactory when we grow up if we acquire any extensive knowledge of the way in which English is actually spoken by people by and large, or if we follow English back through its history. The first thing that will strike us is the fact that a good num-ber of the purist rules appear to be of the nature of re-vealed truth, for it is impossible to arrive at them by any induction from facts. Take, for example, the rule that when we have corresponding pairs of adjectives and ad-verbs, the adverbs end in *-ly*, and that consequently "slow" is an adjective and "slowly" an adverb. The rule does not define the usage of the vernacular, in which the adverbial use of "slow" instead of "slowly" is almost universal. ("Take it slow now!"—can any one imagine a man who was deeply interested in the result saying "Take it slowly"?) It does not define the best literary usage: Shakespeare and Milton and Byron and Thackeray appear not to have heard of it. And it is unsupported by the history of the language. If you go back to the English of the fourteenth century you find our *-ly* ap-pearing as *-liche*, and you realize that it is somehow con-nected with our word "like." (We still make compounds of much the same sort: "business-like," "workman-like.") If you go back still further, say to the ninth or tenth cen-tury, you will find what is going to become this ending occurring on both adjectives and adverbs in the forms re-spectively of *-līc* and *-līce*. You will realize then that the adverbial ending in Old English was simply *-e*. The adjective might have two forms, *slāw* or *slāwlīc*, and the adverb two, *slāwe* or *slāwlīce*. When, in the fifteenth century, all final -*e*'s in English ceased to be pronounced, the historical distinction between adjectives and adverbs disappeared. But by one of those selective principles of language which can be catalogued but not explained, the adjectival ending -*līc* became comparatively inactive in Old English times, whereas the adverbial ending -*līce* remained vigorous, and was frequently added to simple adjectives without the intervention of the corresponding compound adjective. When the final *e* (the former sign of the adverb) disappeared, -*ly* continued to be added freely to adjectives to form adverbs, and consequently became the normal sign of the adverb in modern English. But a good many of the old compound adjectives persisted: friendly, goodly, lovely. And so did a number of the old short adverbs. "Fast" is one; no one has ever maintained, I think, that it is incorrect to say "Go fast." "Hard" is another. "I hit him hard" means something different from "I hardly hit him." When you say "Go slow," you are not employing an adjective or a clipped form of "slowly." You are using an English form of the adverb that has been in continuous use for at least four hundred and fifty years. It might be argued that what the purist rule really means is that it would be better to make our practice with regard to adverbs quite symmetrical and consistent, and abolish adverbs like "slow," "hard," and "wide." But then we run into another rule, the rule against new formations. "Slowly," "hardly," "widely" exist and are unexceptionable, but could we in cold blood recommend "fastly" and "muchly"? And if not, why fuss about "slow"?

Another consideration that must occur to any one who reads books and actually listens to what people say is that the purist standard of correctness is more generous in its damnations than the most rigorous Calvinism ever was. Only written discourse rises to its demands, and only a part of that, as we have seen, can achieve election. Take the case of "whom." "Whom," both relative and interrogative, appears to have become in America a purely literary word. We can employ it on the written page without self-consciousness, but I venture to assert that even college professors who use it in speech do so with deliberate attention and the frantic hope (often misplaced) that after committing themselves to "whom" they have got the proper preposition or transitive verb into the sentence. The vernacular has dispensed with "whom" altogether, either omitting it (which one can frequently do when the "whom" is a relative), or substituting "that" (which has the virtue of being indeclinable) or "who": The man I saw, The man that I saw, The man who I saw. The tendency is even more irresistible when the "whom" stands in the part of the sentence where one usually finds the subject: Who did you see? Listen to the conversation even of cultured people and note how seldom you hear them say "Whom did you see" or "I don't know whom you mean" or "He had no notion whom they were talking about" or "The man whom I saw." There are functions for which full dress and a white tie are *de rigeur* and society will look with disfavor on the man who turns up at them in a business suit, however neat. "Whom," if not a white-tie word, is at least one of a considerable degree of formality. But brief observation must convince any one that in actual practice there are many levels of acceptable English: a level for formal written discourse and formal oratory, a level for somewhat more informal and conversational discourse such as that I am now indulging in, a level for ordinary conversation, and so on. At the formal level I should write "whom" and should insist that all my students should write "whom," but at the conversational level I should say "I don't know who you mean," and I hope I should do it unconsciously.

To any one who has turned an attentive ear to the speech actually holden of men and has further fortified himself by some historical study of the language, the question must sooner or later occur, Where did the rules come from? How did purist critics arrive at them? We know that for a long, long time English was spoken without the benefit of any grammars at all. The grammarians must have started at some point with the existing language, codified it, and erected the rules on the basis of what they found. We shall discover, however, if we pursue the subject, that they did not come to the task without prepossessions. They had Latin grammars, and so far as they could they adapted the categories and terminology of Latin grammar to their English material. Latin by that time was a dead language to which static and absolute rules could be applied with some success. But is it certain that the categories of a language that is not very closely related to English will be appropriate when applied to English? And what logic underlies the attempt to fix as absolutely correct a standard of usage for a living tongue?

There is another attitude towards language which may be called the scientific or historical. It recognizes the fact

that English grammar and usage have always been changing, and it sees no reason to suppose that they will not
continue to do so. Old English was as highly inflected as
modern German. To a purist of the Old English period
our modern distinction between "he," "his," and "him"
would have seemed a puny one. He would have wanted a
dative case as well as a nominative, a genitive, and an accusative, and he would have charged us (quite justly) with
mixing up the cases he bequeathed to us. ("Him" is historically a dative, not an accusative; "you" is historically
a dative, not a nominative.) He would have wanted to
know by what right we drop the endings by which he
nicely distinguished weak adjectives from strong adjectives
and plural adjectives from singular adjectives. He would
ask us where we picked up our barbarous method of asking
questions and indicating negation by the auxiliary "do"
("I don't know" instead of "I know not"; "Do I dare?"
instead of "Dare I?") The purist, I suspect, generally regards Old English as a foreign language, and so avoids
this difficulty. But Chaucer, who wrote in the fourteenth
century, almost in Modern English times, would have
made many of the same strictures. He uses "him" as accusative, but he never uses "you" as nominative; he pre-
serves to a considerable extent the distinction between
weak and strong adjectives and between singular and plural
strong adjectives. He knows how to ask a question with
the auxiliary "do," but he has never heard of using the
same auxiliary in negation. Even the revisers of the King
James Bible, which is only three hundred years old and is
often held up as our model of elevated style, would have
considered our best formal grammar casual and vulgar.

They never used the possessive "its" (neither, apparently, did Shakespeare, and of course not Chaucer), they avoided the periphrastic "do," and they usually distinguished precisely between "ye" (nominative) and "you" (objective): "No doubt but ye are the people, and wisdom shall die with you." Those who have observed how "you," originally a dative, took over the functions of the accusative in Old English times and the functions of the nominative as late as the early seventeenth century are not going to be profoundly shocked at evidence that "who" has for a long time been both accusative and nominative in the vernacular, and in certain constructions is already acceptable as accusative in cultured speech at any level below that of formal written discourse. What this means is that there is a strong tendency in Modern English to substitute for the old method of indicating subject and object relation by inflected forms a method of indicating the same thing by fixed word order.

Those who hold the relativistic attitude do not scorn grammar; far from it. They have written the most learned and useful grammars we have. But they hold that the function of grammar is to describe precisely and in detail what is actually going on in a language at a given period, not to prescribe usage. "A Grammar book," says one of the most respected scholars of the English language (H. C. Wyld), "does not attempt to teach people how they ought to speak, but on the contrary, unless it is a very bad or a very old work, it merely states how, as a matter of fact, certain people do speak at the time at which it is written." Usage, they maintain, is the basis of all the correctness there can be in language. This does not mean that they consider one kind of English just as good as another for a given time and a given occasion. The task of speaking or writing well for one who holds this view is really more exacting than it is for the purist, for he has constantly to inquire what usage really is. He will rely of course on the great dictionaries (the Oxford Dictionary and Webster are models of historical scholarship), but as dictionaries cannot be revised often enough to keep fully abreast of usage, he has constantly to ask himself whether the objection he has long trained himself to feel for certain usages can be justified any longer. For example, when he finds a British stylist like Geoffrey Scott using "like" in the sense of "as" ("Do it like I do"), he has to consider whether he will continue to mark that construction as "incorrect." The historical linguist, knowing that acceptable colloquial usages are always winning their way into the formal style, will develop in himself such sympathy for the niceties of the vernacular as to warn him when his formal usage is becoming literary and lifeless.

For the man who takes this attitude believes that the real life of a language is in its vernacular, not in its formal style. The purist holds that the true language, the correct language, *is* the formal style. This is always murdered by the lips of the vulgar, and must be protected from such violence by inviolable rules. The historical scholar is convinced that rules imposed from above have very little ultimate effect on the actual development of a language, and that the formal style, because of its deliberate artificiality and conservatism, is always moribund. The drift of language is, and always has been, determined by the mob, not by the aristocrat; by the illiterate, not the literate.

It is inevitable that this should be so, for the formal style is only the fringe of existing speech; as it were, the nails and hair of language.

The man who holds the historical attitude welcomes development and change in language because he recognizes it as a sign of creation, not of decay. Much of the change, to be sure, is, so far as he can see, purely mechanical and contingent. For example, the tremendous leveling of inflections in the Late Old English period was probably for the greater part due to the fact that in the Germanic group of languages the word accent, which in the parent Indo-European tongue had shifted about freely as in Greek or Sanskrit, became a strong stress accent on the stem. When you have a strong accent on the beginning of a word with a lot of unstressed syllables trailing after it, the unstressed vowels at the end tend to merge in the obscure vowel sound (the final vowel of *china*), with the result that many of your inflectional endings become identical and hence useless. But there is another, and more interesting, kind of development constantly going on in language. It is nothing less than the mysteriously changing sensibility of man finding its adequate expression in the plastic stuff of speech. The historical student of language looks back with gratitude to the day when a great flood of light poured in upon him and he recognized the fact that all speech is art, and that the poetic faculty of fitting the movements of the mind to adequate words is no less the inheritance of the illiterate peasant than it is of Shakespeare.

The man who holds the historical attitude is a relativist. He believes that, by and large, every period of a language worked out a form of speech well suited to its needs. He does not believe it possible to dissociate the style of an epoch from the mind and sensibility of that epoch. To the question, "What was the best English prose style?" he would reply, "They were all good in their time, and can all fill you with delight, but you should not try to imitate them except as an exercise in appreciating them. If you really want a model that may be helpful to you in developing your own style, you had better take a contemporary like Somerset Maugham or Ernest Hemingway."

I have spoken thus far as though one were free to choose between these two opposed attitudes, but I suspect that my tone has indicated a lack of respect for the purist position. I do not, as a matter of fact, believe the purist position as ordinarily stated to be logically defensible. It accepts relativism up to a certain point and then shifts to absolutism. The purist does not seem to realize that if he appeals to history, he is lost, for history shows all living languages changing continuously, not merely in vocabulary but also in grammatical structure. It is hard to see any principle other than self-flattery underlying the assumption that language develops from a crude and imperfect state up to a stage of perfection at which it should be fixed by unalterable rules. An even greater logical difficulty is presented by the fact that the rules prove on examination to be anything but unalterable. Is any present-day purist shocked by the words "reliable" and "scientist"? They have been in general use less than a hundred years and were long contested. Do twentieth-century purists condemn a construction like the passive progressive "A house is being built"? It has not been found in any printed source earlier than 1769, and appears not to have been recognized in any English grammar before 1802. The purist position is generally in fact merely the expression of a conservative attitude in language, the hardening into dogma of a definition of good taste that consists in part of valid analyses of the structure of accepted contemporary style at the formal level, in part of valid analyses of obsolete or obsolescent formal style, in part of traditional arbitrary vetoes that were never based on the usage of the "best" writers of any period (e.g., the rule against "different than"), and in part of pure whim.

The purist position can be made logically respectable only by assumptions which few of the purists I know are willing to make: assumptions involving theological and moral absolutes. If you can believe with Archbishop Trench that the power of naming things and expressing their relations was a perfect divine gift bestowed on Adam which degenerated when man lost grace; if you can believe that "with every impoverishing and debasing of personal or national life there goes hand in hand a corresponding impoverishment and debasement of language"; if you can believe (and here is the real crux) that by some sort of revelation the right form of language has been indicated and that by teaching it dogmatically you can increase man's moral stature—then you have, I think, an arguable case. My difficulty is that I cannot persuade myself of the revelation and that consequently the whole argument seems to me merely to say that as men get better they find words to fit their improved state. But it also seems to me that as they get worse they find proper words, too: in short, that language at all periods is a marvelously complex and resourceful instrument for expressing the mind of man, whatever the moral state of man's mind may be. It is obvious, of course, that language at one place or in one period, as compared with language at another place or in another period is poorer in ways of expressing certain things, but it is equally obvious that it is richer in ways of expressing other things. The linguistic absolutist will reply that the gain is chiefly in the power to express sin, sloth, and perversity, and with many of his strictures on the moral state of the people speaking the language I shall agree. But will he really come down to cases and show the moral superiority or inferiority of expressing grammatical relations by fixed word order rather than by inflectional endings? Is the elimination of grammatical gender in English a sign of debasement or the contrary? Is "different from" *morally* superior to "different than"? Can he really write a persuasive history of the English language on theological principles?

It may, I think, be safely stated that there are at the present day no competent students of the history of the English language who hold the purist position. The battle has been fought and won, though it will be long before the good textbooks—of which there are now many—eliminate the bad ones; long before it becomes accepted as a matter of course that the teacher who plans to deal with matters of grammar and usage will first equip himself with some knowledge of the history of English. In linguistics it is hard to believe that relativitism has not come to stay.

There are two attitudes in criticism which may be called respectively the dogmatic and the historical. Underlying the dogmatic position are always two assumptions expressed or implied: the first, that there exist canons, rules, or methods for judging absolutely the worth of literature; the second, that the critic, ideally at least, can apply these measures without error. It is only fair to add that dogmatic criticism admits in a practical way that very few critics *have* applied the measures accurately. As a general thing critics of this stamp feel sure that nearly all critics who have preceded them were disqualified by prejudices and superstitions due to the times in which they lived, or by defects of temperament. Similarly, it appears that the measures adopted have varied remarkably from age to age: from the neo-classical "rules" of "correctness," reasonableness, and moral edification to the modern "rules" of concentration, irony, and coherence of images. If you have any doubt as to what I mean, read what Dr. Johnson has to say on metaphysical poetry in his *Life of Cowley* and then read the analysis of Marvell's *Definition of Love* in the currently popular textbook by Brooks and Warren, *Understanding Poetry*. The "rules" of the dogmatic critic have never had the historical continuity that formal grammar has given to the rules of the purist, and not all dogmatic critics are conservatives, but the positions of the two are still fundamentally the same. Both believe that there are measures applicable to all poetry or all language, regardless of when it was written, and both believe that the critic, or at least they themselves, can apply these measures.

Dogmatic criticism, in one guise or another, has held the field from the beginning. The results are at once very interesting and very discouraging. Because of the shifting nature of the measures employed, the judgments of our critics do not merely seem to contradict one another; they contradict and repeat one another like the curves of an ascending spiral. Dr. Johnson is patronizing in his treatment of the metaphysicals. He measures them by the practice of Dryden and Pope, and announces that their method was, on the whole, vicious. Wordsworth, and after him Arnold and Housman, patronize Dryden and Pope, denying them in fact the name of poets. Though all three would have qualified their praise of the metaphysicals because of what they would have called their "extravagances," they would have been at one in feeling that there was more poetry in a square inch of Donne or Marvell than in a square mile of Pope. Our contemporary critics —Mr. Ransom, Mr. Brooks, Mr. Warren—make metaphysical poetry literally the measure of excellence, think pretty well of Dryden and Pope, and consider Romantic poetry the accursed thing. The whipping boy of criticism was once Donne, then he was Pope. Now he is Shelley.

There is another attitude in criticism which I shall call the relativistic or historical. It questions the possibility of absolute critical judgments because it finds no evidence in history that a permanent standard measure can be devised for literature, or that it could be applied without error if it were devised. It believes that the poetry of every age is the expression of, or expresses itself through, the sensibility of that age. This sensibility represents the temporary and precarious stabilization of the extremely complex organism of the mind. It suffers extraordinary shifts at given historical points, and it is these shifts that mark off the "periods" in literature. If one considers the rules or standards which each age has advanced for the evaluation of literature, one will find that instead of being objective and permanent, they are merely the definition of the sensibility of that age.

The critic who subscribes to the historical position is very loath to admit that poetry has ever got off the track, or, to state the same thing in a different way, that there ever was a prolonged period of general bad taste. He sees that there have been many sensibilities, each with its appropriate expression in literature, but he does not select one of them as "right" or "good" and condemn the others as "wrong" or "bad." He considers the question as to what constitutes a "right" sensibility meaningless, as meaningless as it would be in physics to ask what constitutes a "right" frame of reference. Good taste in literature he defines as he would good taste in language, that is, the expression of sensibility in accordance with the accepted usage of the time. Poets throughout the ages have not, in his opinion, been working at the same problem. Each age has a unique problem, and each age has solved that problem as well as it could be solved.

The historical critic believes that no poetry which had the acclaim of respectable judges in the past can possibly have been without "feeling." He believes that Pope raised as powerful feelings in Johnson as Blake does in us. If Pope rouses no such feelings in us, it is not because he is a bad poet; it is because sensibility has shifted since that time, because our sensibility is organized in such a way as to make much of his poetry inaccessible to us.

The historical critic believes that all original criticism is subjective: the description of the impact of the work on his own historically limited sensibility. He does not for that reason conclude that there is no permanent value in his critical judgments. The fact that his measurement is relative does not make it any less a valid measurement: he must merely measure carefully and report his frame of reference. His frame of reference is his own sensibility, which to a very great extent is that of his age, or at least of his generation. He can indicate it by abundant example (the poems or passages he really likes best) or by theory (the formal structure which seems to him to produce the most "poetic" results). If he experiences profound physiological disturbances constantly when he reads Blake and seldom when he reads Pope, he will record that as a very significant fact, but he will not conclude that his predecessors who report other experiences in reading Pope had bad taste, nor will he try to persuade himself that he is really getting out of Pope what they did. *He grants the general, though relative, validity of all honest critical judgments.* He knows that as he has his own areas of great sensitivity, he has also critical blind spots and critical deafnesses. All these different records of successful and unsuccessful reading go together to make up the criticism of a poem. To his own judgment of Pope he adds not only those of Housman and Arnold, but also those of Byron and Johnson.

The historical critic's most rewarding task and his most serious responsibility lie in the evaluation of contemporary literature. Sensibility is always in the process of shifting. Every sensibility finally achieves its idiom, its perfectly adequate expression. But the idiom is not achieved all at once. There can always be heard in every age the discord of creation, the sharp, original voices of men triumphantly working their will on language to make it fit *their* thoughts, not the thoughts of their fathers. It is the function of the critic, in literature no less than in language, to recognize and define the emergent idiom. He may not be able to *like* it, any more than he likes innovations in the personal pattern of speech which he has with difficulty mastered. He will not consider, when he is writing as a critic, that his personal likings have much to do with the matter.

> Say neither . . .
> "It is a deadly magic and accursed,"
> Nor, "It is blest," but only "It is here."

I do not think that the opponents of critical relativism realize how much their own systems are infected with the relativistic principle, or how doctrinaire and forbidding they would have to make them to achieve logical coherence. In dealing with the mind of the artist, we are all relativists. Absolutists join with relativists in seeing Shakespeare not as a mind divorced from the limitations of history, but as a practical dramatist working within the sensibility of the Elizabethan age. There is also a growing agreement to consider taste as identical in its nature with genius: to suppose that if we read poetry with pleasure, it is because we possess, though in a more passive form, the faculty which enabled the poet to write his poems. Logic points inexorably to the conclusion that if the more imperious and original manifestation of the faculty is conditioned by time, so is the more passive: that there is no more basis for supposing that a critic can make absolute judgments than there is for thinking that poets can write poetry that will never need historical justification. And our absolutist critics, as a matter of fact, find it easy enough to draw that conclusion for all critics except themselves.

VIII

DOGMA, SCIENCE,
AND POETRY

Few people nowadays really like dogma. Mr. T. E. Hulme once said that he accepted the sentiment of the Church for the sake of the dogma, thereby implying that he had a natural appetite for dogma and a natural repugnance to sentiment. He was probably sincere, but the statement on most men's lips would rightly be regarded as a paradox, for the prevailing temper of our times is favorable to religious sentiment of all kinds and unfavorable to dogma. We instinctively like the exalted feelings associated with the practice or contemplation of religion. To nearly all of us, no matter how much we believe in it, dogma presents grave and recurring difficulty.

Science and art being recognized and respectable categories, we try to escape from our difficulty by bringing dogma in under one or the other. Clergymen who respect science try to save dogma by linking it to physics. Scientists who respect religion vindicate its dogma by equating it with poetry. The result of either tactic is to destroy dogma altogether. The view which I have taken in what follows is that dogma is most important and must be preserved; and that in order to preserve it we must know in what it differs from science and from poetry.

If we oppose the attempt to save dogma by making it a department of science, we would seem to be forced to defend the opposed thesis that dogma has nothing whatever to do with science, is not concerned with it, does not touch it at any point. We must be careful not to allow ourselves to take that stand without some qualification, for it has the look of pure obscurantism. Christian dogmas, by and large, are autonomous with regard to science; but science does impinge upon them in one area which is of vital importance.

I

Science is naturalistic in its scope; dogma is not. If we are to understand that, we must pause and define what we mean by the term "nature." Nature, in the widest sense, is everything that exists or has being, as it is in itself, not as it appears in the constructions of a human mind. Science postulates nature in this sense, but does not profess to know anything about it. If there be a God, He is part of nature in this widest definition.

In the second and more restricted sense, nature is all that is given to (*data*), or, as Kant more truly perceived, made by (*facta*), the human mind. We are not passive machines which nature, in the first sense, operates. Nature makes impressions on us. From these impressions the mind *constructs* the world as we know it. Color, we are aware, is not a quality of an object but a sensation in the brain. There is something in the object capable of absorbing a portion of the spectrum when white light falls on it; the unabsorbed rays are reflected on the retina, and the resulting sensation in the brain we call "red." We unconsciously project this sensation into the object, though the object is only partially responsible for it. An easy way to test this is to look again, this time using light that contains no "red" rays. The object has not been changed in the least, but we shall now see it as black.

In the same way it is obvious that sounds are not "things in themselves," but sensations in the brain. It is not so obvious that volume and mass as we perceive them in bodies are not qualities of things in themselves. A little reflection, however, will show that, like color and sound, they too are constructions of our minds, built up from the sense of touch and from muscular sensations.

We can go on to still more disquieting conclusions. Space and time, which seem so completely independent of humanity, are not absolute qualities of things in themselves but mental categories, frames into which the *facta* of experience must be fitted before they make any kind of sense.

Nature in the second meaning mentioned above is a selection made from nature in this first meaning of the word. It is that portion of existing things which the human mind is capable of apprehending. Rather, it is the sum of the constructions which the human mind puts upon things so apprehended. If there be a God, He will still remain in this kind of nature. My illustrations happen all to be restricted to constructions of the senses recognized by the kind of nature I am about to describe, but to maintain at this point that those senses are our *only* avenues of knowledge would be unwarranted.

Nature in a third, and still more restricted, meaning is that portion of nature in the second sense on which all men are agreed insofar as they are sane and normal. It is the realm of "natural law." It is the part of nature which is of the greatest *immediate* importance, for we must observe its ways if we are to live at all. Men may not agree upon a point in theology or upon the value of a given piece of poetry. They do agree that if you touch fire, you will be burned; that if you are long submerged in water, you will drown; that if you leap from a tall building, you will be dashed to pieces. This is the realm of science, in the gross or popular sense. It is of *general* application, and takes from individual experience only so much as is applicable to all men. In most problems that face mankind, it has no room for the individual.

The God of historical Christianity, a reality not apprehended by all men in an invariable fashion, is excluded from "nature" at exactly this point. When we speak of a philosophy or method as "materialistic," "mechanistic," or "naturalistic," we are using an imperfect nomenclature to indicate that the conception of nature employed excludes everything not found in nature *in this third sense.*

Nature in the fourth sense is a still narrower selection from nature in the second sense, and consists of only so much of Sense III as theoretical science needs for its constructions. Matter here loses its "common sense" attributes of density, color, mass, etc., and becomes a swarm of invisible electric particles. Science here tends towards the austere and completely abstract constructions of mathematics. There are undoubtedly metaphysical assumptions underlying this kind of science, but since the materials on which they operate are those of nature in Sense III, they are incapable of being developed into theology. And this final sort of "nature," or *theoretical* science, rests on unprovable postulates most readily illustrated by the axioms in geometry.

II

What precedes has been dull reading; but I hope that all those who propose to follow me through the remainder of this essay have tried to peruse it. We constantly meet the statement that science is a selection, or abstraction, from the fullness of reality. My experience indicates that that phrase is pretty much meaningless until one has been conducted through some such scheme as that which I have outlined, and has seen the rich welter of human experience—its hopes, its fears, its loves, its ecstasies, its despairs, it colors, its tones, its feeling—all stripped down to the beautifully clear, but cold and impersonal, constructions of theoretical science.

The selection does not (and this is important) proceed by mapping off certain areas and excluding them as beyond the domain of science. It proceeds rather by a rarefication or a stripping down. If we think of nature in Sense II as a square, nature in Sense III is not a smaller square marked off within its boundaries. The domain of theoretical science is coextensive with all human experience, but within that area it ignores all but a small fraction of what it finds.

Science achieves its beautiful clarity and precision by deliberately excluding, at the very beginning, everything that will not fit into the final pattern. I am not surprised when laymen with no training in science are depressed by the triumphant emergence of a scientist from an argument in which everything is explained and God left out;[1] but I am indeed surprised when I occasionally see scientists themselves exhilarated by such tugging at their bootstraps. Of course God is left out. He was left out by definition, at the very outset. There can be a "scientific" description, or explanation, of anything; but no one should suppose that such an explanation—though true—exhausts the object.

Yet we must avoid setting boundaries to the scientific method and saying, "Up to this point science may operate, but no further." There are no such boundaries. The proper procedure is not to deny the right of science to push its inquiries out to any limits it chooses, but to evaluate the results of its inquiries in terms of our *total* experience. Not, "This is false," but, "This seems to contain no logical fallacy, *but what of it?*"

Arguments from science to religious sanctions are very dangerous and should invariably be avoided by those who have not had a considerable training in science. In spite of what one reads in popular books on religion, the theory

---

[1] That is, the creative, personal, supernatural God of Christian theology. As much of God as can be comprised in the concepts of the ultimate intelligibility and harmony of experience is kept in, but He is now called "the structure of the universe" or "natural law" and—as handled by science—is not in any proper sense a *religious* entity. The postulates of science can be *developed* into a "natural theology," but such development, if rigorous, can never end in the positions of Christian theology. And even natural theology is a different kind of logical structure from science. The scientist can ignore it completely.

of relativity makes belief in God no easier than it was before. It also makes it no harder. It just has nothing to do with belief in God. Electricity has nothing to do with the doctrine of the Communion of Saints. The arrogance of irreligious science is often blamed in our time. The devout should be quite as much concerned with the ignorant use of popular science in theological discussion.

Christian theology very obviously rests on unprovable postulates—the statements of the Creed. Many Christians worry constantly over the fact that they are unprovable. Theoretical science also rests on unprovable postulates, but few people worry about them. They seem, as we say, "self-evident." Why is this?

It is, I think, because of the operation of what I may call "mental climate." Every age has its mental climate, the effect of which is to make men unconscious of the postulates they make in that field of endeavor to which the mental climate is favorable. The mental climate of the modern world is favorable to the development of theoretical science. Hence with no hesitation or anxiety we make the postulates demanded by science. Furthermore, the effect of mental climate is to cause us to arrogate for one (and only one) kind of human thought, the function of dealing with "truth" or "reality." The natural temper of our minds now is scientific. It is scientific partly because of specific early training, partly because of the pressure of a general habit of mind which affects us without our being aware of it. Without being taught to do so, we assign all "truth" to the province of science. Whatever science cannot manipulate we feel to be unreal or untrue.

Now, we have plenty of evidence that there have been

eras during which the mental climate was favorable to metaphysics and theology, and unfavorable to natural science. In this connection, the Gnostic heresy, at the very beginning of the Christian church, is most enlightening. The Gnostics were repelled by the historical element in Christianity, and repudiated it in favor of a purely metaphysical and mystical belief.

Or consider the "science" of the Middle Ages, in which the passion for placing everything in the deductive framework of Christian theology completely dominated the will to collect, to analyze, and to experiment. Every text of Scripture, no matter how prosaic a statement of historical fact, was given not one, but three allegorical meanings. Every object in nature had a spiritual significance, more important than its material content.

The bestiaries are the natural-history texts of the period. In them purely fabulous animals such as the unicorn and the onocentaur are presented as seriously as the goat or the stag, and hardly a real animal escapes without fabulous traits. The elephant has only one joint in his legs and must sleep leaning against a tree; to capture him you saw the tree partly through. Once he has fallen on his side, he cannot get up again. The weasel is bisexual; it impregnates itself in the mouth and the young are born through the ear. And so on. How could men be content to remain so ignorant of ascertainable facts? Because they were "making sense" of nature in a framework (the theological) which interested them more than the scientific. Every one of those animals had a theological meaning. They were types of Christ, Adam, Eve, the Blessed Virgin, the Devil. What the author was concerned with was the ingenious exposition of the allegory inherent in the traits of the animals. Those traits he was content to take on hearsay.

Let us not be too quick to smile at him. Our own solemn satisfaction with attempts to explain the entire range of existence in terms of a materialistic philosophy are probably just as absurd. The view now current that *our* mental climate came to us by a long and painful growth in which the race passed from mental adolescence to mental maturity is probably self-flattery. Every previous age has likewise made the calm assumption that *its* mental climate represented mental maturity, and apparently with just as good reason.

History rather suggests that the scientific temper is not the result of a gradual and progressive growth of the mind, but that it came suddenly and inexplicably by a shift of mental organization, and that it may depart as suddenly and inexplicably. Where is the evidence of a gradual development of the scientific temper from Aristotle to Archimedes to Francis Bacon and Galileo? Is it not clear that the ancient Greeks could have made every discovery in science on which we pride ourselves, if they had thought it worth while?

One remembers that famous quotation from Seneca, which Macaulay quotes so appositely in his essay on Bacon:

"In my own time there have been inventions of this sort, transparent windows, tubes for diffusing warmth equally through all parts of a building, shorthand, which has been carried to such a perfection that a writer can keep pace with the most rapid speaker. But the inventing of such things is drudgery for the lowest slaves; philosophy lies deeper. It is not her office to teach men how to use their hands. The object of her lessons is to form the soul."

The fact is that Aristotle (in his biological work, not in his metaphysics) and Archimedes were not typical of Greek mentality as a whole, which held experimentation in contempt as involving manual labor, and devoted itself wholeheartedly to only one science—mathematics. All through the Middle Ages a theological climate reigned. Then suddenly—overnight as it were—the modern temper was born. There has been no real progression in it since Galileo; only an enormously fruitful extension of it in human life.

There are two principles which we need to master and to practice constantly. The first is very simple and is clear to any one the instant it is pointed out; the other is much more difficult, though to our children it will probably be a commonplace.

To begin with the easy one: science of today (science of yesterday was even worse) is often guilty of what some one has called the "nothing-but fallacy"—that is, of consciously or unconsciously assuming that a scientific description of an object exhausts it. Love between man and woman can be explained in terms of glandular secretions, and the explanation will be true. It is then assumed that "love is *nothing but* glands," which is a fallacy. Other examples will readily occur: "a rainbow is nothing but sunlight refracted by raindrops"; "poetry is nothing but the association of images"; "history is nothing but the operation of economic forces."

As we have seen, science achieves its precision and coherence by rigorous *selection* from the matter of experience. It excludes by definition nine-tenths of any individual experience. Its constructions are inevitably mechanistic or mathematical because it has sorted over its materials at the outset and has rejected all those that will not fit into a mechanistic or mathematical scheme.

Now, our mental climate causes us to assume that the materials which it rejects are not "real." They are just as real as the others, and often, so far as you and I are concerned, of greater importance. Science is never in a position to claim totality. After the scientist has finished, there is just as much room as before for a different or complementary description. Both may be true, though no logic can reconcile them.

That brings me to the second principle. I follow Mr. T. E. Hulme in calling it the principle of discontinuity. Theology and science are not different areas of a single continuum, like the bands of long and short waves in the spectrum. They are discontinuous. They do not operate in different territories, which may be bridged by logic. They operate in the same territory, but they are logically irreconcilable.

It requires a good deal of a mental wrench to grasp this notion, and I doubt if our generation will ever be at home in it. The scientists take to it much more readily than the rest of us. It is possible here to give only analogies, for occasional and temporary logical discontinuity within the naturalistic system is of course a different thing from the total discontinuity I have in mind. But such analogies may help to make my position clear. Consider first the matter of Euclidean and non-Euclidean geometry. We *know* instinctively that the Euclidean geometry is of the essence of things. When we say that a straight line is the shortest distance between two points, or that through a given point in a plane only one parallel to a given line can be drawn, we do not feel in the least as though we were postulating something. But we are. Both statements are incapable of proof, and it is only habit and mental climate which makes them seem "self-evident."

Our scientists now have geometries based on the equally legitimate assumptions that a curve is the shortest distance between two points, and that through a given point any number of parallels can be drawn. They are not mere intellectual playthings, but are the kind of geometry used in relativity theory, one of the most fruitful achievements of modern physics. When applied to some of the data of experience, they prove to be more "true" than the Euclidean propositions. For a time these new geometries seemed totally discontinuous from Euclidean geometry, but the discontinuity has now been bridged to general satisfaction. Euclidean geometry, mathematicians say, is a special case of the curved-space geometry: it is for all practical purposes "true" if the distances and areas it deals with are relatively small—i.e., small on the cosmic scale. The plane which Euclidean geometry postulates is not furnished by nature, but a small portion of a very large spherical surface is remarkably like a plane.

It is possible, however, to instance a genuine and very important case of unresolved logical discontinuity in physics. Newton considered light to be a stream of weightless particles, and that view was considered satisfactory by physicists for over a century. This particle or corpuscular theory of light broke down and was discarded when it failed to explain phenomena of diffraction. What happens in diffraction is that light *bends* around very small obstacles, something that a stream of particles cannot be supposed to do. A wave *can* bend around obstacles. Since all the other phenomena that had then been observed could be explained by the theory that light consists of very short electromagnetic waves, and this theory further gave a very satisfactory explanation of diffraction, the wave theory completely displaced the particle theory, which was held to be dead and buried. The quantum physics of this century has reopened the whole question. To give one example, it was found that when homogeneous light (in "wave" terminology, light all of the same wave length) impinges on a metal surface, electrons are extracted from the metal and speed away with a certain velocity. On the wave theory, the velocity of the electrons must increase with the intensity of the light. But as a matter of fact it does not. A more intense light extracts *more* electrons, but their velocity is not increased. Newton's theory again revives, for if light were a stream of energy units ("photons")—a sophisticated but recognizable version of his "corpuscles"—that is just what we should expect.

Physicists of the present day are using both theories. There are phenomena which can be explained by the quantum theory but not by the wave theory. There are phenomena which can be explained by the wave theory but not by the quantum theory. And there are phenomena that can be explained equally well by either. It has been flippantly said that physicists now treat light as a wave motion on Monday, Wednesday, and Friday, and as a stream of particles on Tuesday, Thursday, and Saturday.

The quantum theory and the wave theory are definitely not modifications of a single hypothesis. It is not merely that the mechanical models we construct in our minds for each concept are different; the abstract mathematics of wave mechanics and quantum mechanics are different. They are logically irreconcilable, discontinuous. *But they both work.* By using the particle theory on certain occasions the scientist can "make sense" of a mass of data which the wave theory is impotent to organize, and can make predictions which experiment verifies, and *vice versa.*

This state of discontinuity, since it occurs within the naturalistic scheme itself and involves no disparity in the elements of nature considered, will perhaps yield to the attack of a more comprehensive theory. Indeed Einstein, if I understand correctly a popular book he published in 1938, finds a tenable reconciliation of the difficulties in the principle of indeterminacy and "probability waves," though he is not sure that a better solution may not be found. It makes little difference for my purpose. Logical discontinuity of the most acute sort at least *did* exist in physics for many years, and was met by the sensible course of using the discontinuous systems in turn for the purposes which experience showed them to be useful for. It is easier, of course, if you can convince yourself, as most physicists apparently do with their puzzles, that the discontinuity is merely temporary—an interim state. I entertain no such hope for the kind of discontinuity I am talking about. Because of my conviction on the one hand of the transcendental and supernatural character of truth, and on the other of the naturally limited powers of the human mind, I accept philosophical discontinuity as forever the lot of man, no matter how far he may go in solving particular puzzles; and I want men to make full-hearted use of disparate systems even if they cannot see how they go together. And as evidence that such an attitude of mind is possible, I instance the physicists' simultaneous use of the incompatible hypotheses of particles and wave motion.

In short, the universe can be embraced by no single human system of thought—nor, for that matter, by all of them together. The notion that science is a caterpillar on the edge of the leaf of the universe, settling down to the comfortable job of eating and digesting it all, is no less fantastic than the medieval belief that the whole universe could be satisfactorily analyzed in the concepts and terminology of a historical theology. Science is a glorious demonstration of the powers of the human mind, and our scientific constructions are undoubtedly the greatest achievement of this age; but science does not make religious dogma either fatuous or unnecessary.

The elements of experience are like pieces of a huge jigsaw puzzle, thrown out before us on a table. As we sort them over, we despair of fitting them into a single pattern. But little by little, we find that we can select one sort of pieces that *will* make a pattern, and another sort that will make another pattern. Finally we can account for a good many of the pieces. That is the best we can expect. For better or for worse, we must face the difficult position of having, treasuring, and using discontinuous systems which long experience has shown to be necessary to a really abundant life.

I have spoken of science and dogma as being "irreconcilable by logic." By that I do not mean that theology is illogical; rather that neither system, no matter how far extended, will ever include the other. They are not so much hostile as incommensurate. I know that many thoughtful people who are attracted to the Christian position feel that they cannot accept it because it is "repugnant to reason." Actually, the dogmas to which they object usually have nothing to do with reason, being postulates prior to any logical construction. The logic of dogmatic Christianity, when it is really a question of logic, is generally held, even by unbelievers, to be very impressive. What the statement "repugnant to reason" really means is that the postulates are felt to be contradictory to the modern or scientific spirit. And so they are, though I should prefer to say "disparate with" rather than "contradictory to." We cannot prove them. Neither can we prove the axioms of science. It is merely our mental climate that makes us acutely aware of the postulates in theology and unconscious of those in science.

We must not expect to dwell in orthodox Christianity without some mental strain. If we examine the first articles of the Nicene Creed, we shall at once agree that they are not "scientific." Take one point that is particularly illuminating: Jesus Christ is said to have been begotten of His Father "before all worlds." Now science knows nothing of any event that happened "before all worlds." It may assign fantastic antiquity to an event; but it can never say, "This event happened out of all time." The statement that God the Father made all things by the Son can never be brought within the domain of science. Science assumes its kind of world as existing to begin with. It knows nothing of how it came into being.

Yet we must be cautious when we say that science "has nothing to do" with Christian dogma. Christianity is a historical religion, and the whole central portion of the Creed consists of statements that either are true in the scientific sense or are not true in any sense at all. That Jesus Christ came down from Heaven for us men and for our salvation, and that He was incarnate by the Holy Ghost, are statements which science must decline to investigate. But that He was born of a virgin, that He suffered under Pontius Pilate, was crucified, dead, and buried—those statements are in the domain of science, and so also is the statement that after being dead three days He returned to life again, if by it is meant no more than the words seem literally to convey.

Science, of course, cannot now actually investigate the alleged virgin birth of Christ, nor His physical resurrection; but as those are events which, if they happened at all, happened within the framework of science's own kind of nature, it can legitimately subject them to its own kind of interpretation. The conclusion is inevitable because of the restriction of the premises. Since we have no scientifically authenticated record of a human being born without a human father, since we have no scientifically authenticated record of a human being who rose from the dead—or to change the language, since our experimental generalizations indicate overwhelmingly that the sexual union of father and mother is necessary for the procreation of a child and that the functions of life are not restored after sufficient time has elapsed for *rigor mortis* to ensue, there is (speaking scientifically), a very high degree of probability that these events did not take place as the Creed says they did.

Notice that I say "a very high degree of probability." In the rough and ready generalizations of everyday life, we would say, "It is certain that these events did not take place." That is not scientific. True science must envisage the possibility of even such extraordinary happenings. Some of the lower animals (e.g., frogs.) are, or may be, produced from unfertilized ova. Recent experimentation with dogs has shown that life can be restored after a longer period of "death" than was formerly thought possible. But all this is not of the slightest comfort to those who wish to buttress their theology by science. If science decided that Jesus was born of a virgin, it would classify the event as "parthenogenesis," an extremely rare but quite *natural* occurrence. *You cannot start from naturalistic premises and arrive at supernatural sanctions;* and the sooner writers on religion realize it, the better.

It is this fact—that Christian dogma, in the main wholly outside the domain of science, does impinge upon science in one crucial area—which causes dogma to present such grave difficulties. It may be some comfort to realize, however, that this state of strain is nothing new. Christian dogma has always felt that strain as purely metaphysical systems have not. I have referred to the Gnostics: how they tried to remove the strain by removing the historical element. Our tendency is to try to remove it by eliminating the supernatural element. There is no finality about either the Gnostic temper of mind or ours.

Our trouble springs from the fact that, being pervaded unconsciously by the scientific temper, we begin with the historical portion of the Creed and work outward. If (we say) Jesus was a man, born of a woman, who died on the cross, it is probable that He was *merely* a man, and did die; and all the rest—about the Persons of the Trinity, the Virgin Birth, the Resurrection, the Ascension, the Last Judgment, even the Catholic and Apostolic Church —is, as Matthew Arnold uncompromisingly maintained, "*Aberglaube*," "fairy tales," "The three Lord Shaftesburys." But nothing obliges us to take the Creed in that order; nor should we ever so take it if our interest is in religion.

We should start with the supernatural portion and come inward. *If* Jesus Christ was begotten by His Father before all worlds, *if* by Him all things were made, then there is nothing surprising in His Virgin Birth, His Resurrection, or His Ascension. That is, we should deliberately—even if we must do violence to our ordinary habits—remove the historical portion of the Creed entirely from the setting of natural science, and place it in the setting of theology, where as part of a system of religion it belongs.

In short, you cannot combine the naturalistic postulates of science with the supernatural postulates of theology. Either you must follow your naturalistic argument unflinchingly to its conclusion, with a result that you will find all the sanctions of Christian theology excluded; or you must frankly accept, by an act of faith, those postulates which assign to the Church a supernatural origin and a supernatural guidance. On that basis Christian dogma is unassailable. On any other it is entitled to no particular respect.

As I re-read this, it seems to me that in my effort to make the principle of discontinuity clear, I have overemphasized the difficulty of living with disparate systems. Science and theology are irreconcilable by logic, but they are reconcilable in conduct. I think of the problem of living as analogous to the problem of a tightrope walker balanced over an abyss. He leans now to one side, now to the other, instinctively, to maintain his balance, but *he gets ahead on the wire*. Of course in the mind of God all our systems are reconcilable and a unity. Their disparateness is merely the measure of our finite natures.

III

Since Christian dogma cannot be fitted into the framework of natural science, the modern mind, if it saves any of that dogma, is apt to do it by identifying dogma with poetry. It will be useful to develop some modern theories of poetry which show this tendency, together with some others that seem to me more useful.

Literature and Dogma is the title of a once-famous book by Matthew Arnold; a book which is still superior, both in style and argument, to other books defending similar positions. Arnold's book is beautifully clear, because, after his habit, he eschewed everything complicated and metaphysical, and chose a positivistic standpoint. Conduct, he says, is three-fourths of life. Religion is no more—and no less—than "morality touched by emotion." The sole concern of the authors of the Old Testament was conduct, or, to use a word "touched by emotion," righteousness. The theology of the Jews was completely unspeculative. God, to the prophets, was "the Eternal, not ourselves, that makes for righteousness." The language of the major books of the Old Testament is the language of poetry, not of metaphysics. It is language "thrown out at a not fully grasped object"—language which makes no pretense of being precise. But this grand and simple religion was obscured by a vast *Aberglaube*.[2] This *Aberglaube* can be seen in such a late book as *Daniel*.

Jesus Christ restored and perfected the original message of Judaism. His concern, like that of the prophets, was with conduct, but He taught a method and revealed a secret. For Him God was no more than "the Eternal, not ourselves, that makes for righteousness." But He taught men the only successful method of being righteous. His language was the vivid language of poetry, not the language of science or of metaphysics. He was "above the heads of his followers," who interpreted as literal what he meant to be figurative. And so, almost immediately, a new *Aberglaube* arose, obscuring the message of Jesus even in the earliest records.

The result was metaphysics and dogma—all, to use Arnold's words, "fairy tales." The dogma of the Atonement is a fairy tale; the doctrine of the Trinity (which Arnold ridiculed indecently in a parable of the three Lords Shaftesbury), worse than a fairy tale. For dogma as dogma Arnold leaves no place whatever. For literature, for poetry, he had, and wished others to have, a consuming pas-

---

[2] *Anglice*, "superstition." Arnold says that he prefers the German word to the English because it has less derogatory coloring.

sion. But the sooner we got rid of Christian dogma (not some dogmas, but all dogma), the better off we should be.

"The reasons [for believing that God is a person who thinks and loves] drawn from metaphysics one dismisses with sheer satisfaction. They have convinced no one, they have given rest to no one, they have given joy to no one. People have swallowed them, people have fought over them, people have shown their ingenuity over them; but no one has ever enjoyed them. Nay, no one has ever really understood them."

With poetry it is a different case.

"The future of poetry is immense, because in poetry, where it is worthy of its high destinies, our race, as time goes on, will find an ever surer and surer stay. There is not a creed which is not shaken, not an accredited dogma which is not shown to be questionable, not a received tradition which does not threaten to dissolve. Our religion has materialized itself in the fact, in the supposed fact; it has attached its emotion to the fact, and now the fact is failing it. But for poetry the idea is everything; the rest is a world of illusion, of divine illusion. Poetry attaches its emotion to the idea; the idea *is* the fact. The strongest part of our religion today is its unconscious poetry."

Arnold himself (if one can trust the language of *Literature and Dogma*, and *God and the Bible*) would have found no "unconscious poetry" in such formularies as the Nicene Creed. The Bible, yes—everywhere, for that is language "thrown out" at an object. But since the intent of the framers of the Creed was to use definite and precise language, he would apparently have held it in contempt. One can see, however, how his position might very easily be extended until dogma was accepted as poetry. I well remember how an intelligent woman once said to me, "I cannot say the Apostles' Creed because it is bare, bald statement of things which I do not believe. But I can recite the Nicene Creed with fervor, because it is such glorious poetry."

The proposal to substitute poetry for dogma is usually indicative of intense moral earnestness. Arnold was a strenuous and sincere moralist. Literature acquired its vast importance for him because it, and it alone, could "touch conduct with emotion." One came to the essential things in life through culture, which is knowing "the best that has been thought and said in the world." No poetry could be called supremely great unless it possessed "high seriousness."

From Arnold we may profitably turn to his slightly younger contemporary, Count Leo Tolstoi. Arnold is the better critic; Tolstoi by far the greater theorist. Indeed, Tolstoi's *What Is Art?* may justly be regarded as the basic work in modern theory of poetry, and one of the three or four most important books of all time in that field. Every one knows how Tolstoi, after having written the great novels on which his fame as an artist rests, underwent a religious conversion, studied and meditated for years over the problem of religion, and when he had settled that, both in theory and practice, turned with equal persistence and vigor to an examination of the problem of art. Like Arnold (and all really modern theorists) he abandons transcendental metaphysics. Art in its essence, he says, is the transmission of feeling, nothing more.

"To evoke in oneself a feeling one has experienced, and having evoked it in oneself, then, by means of movements, lines, colors, sounds, or forms expressed in words, so to transmit the feeling that others may experience the same feeling,—that is the activity of Art."

When we say that art is good, we are really making two judgments, not one. Tolstoi calls these "the judgment of art considered apart from subject matter" and "the judgment according to subject matter." Art is good (effective might be a better word) in the first sense if it succeeds in infecting others with the feeling intended—if it *does* transmit feeling. Tolstoi insists that this kind of goodness must be evaluated quantitatively. The work of art must be generally infectious, must produce its effect upon the unlettered peasant as well as upon the aristocrat. All obscure works, all works appealing only to a class, are in this sense bad art, or rather, they are "counterfeit art," not art at all. (His prime examples of counterfeit art are the operas of Wagner and the writings of the French symbolist poets.)

Art is good in the second sense if the feeling transmitted is good; and to be good it must be in accord with the best religious perception of its time. The religious perception of our time is "the consciousness that our well-being, both material and spiritual, individual and collective, temporal and eternal, lies in the growth of brotherhood among all men—in their loving harmony with one another." In proportion as he repudiates the orthodox sanctions of Christianity, he assigns a high place to art. "Art is not a pleasure, a solace, or an amusement; art is a great matter. Art is an organ of human life, transmitting man's reasonable perception into feeling." And only as man's "reasonable perception" is transformed into feeling does he do the things he should.

It is easy, because of their intense moral earnestness, to group Arnold and Tolstoi. I wish to add a third to the company: Mr. I. A. Richards. A hasty reading of his *Principles of Literary Criticism* would probably not lead one to make that association, for he has seen fit to present his system with a flippancy which belies his real seriousness. But moralist he is; and he makes for poetry claims as resounding as do Arnold and Tolstoi. Richard's method is psychological. As one would expect, his philosophy is materialistic and his ethics utilitarian. At the base of his system lies what he believes to be a purely psychological theory of value. Metaphysical sanctions are dismissed as unnecessary. Morals are regarded as purely prudential: we do not avoid doing a thing because it is forbidden but because, on the whole, we shall lose more by the action than we shall gain. The human mind is a systematization of impulses—or to confine ourselves to the positive expression of impulses—our minds are, at any given moment, a swarm of "appetencies," each one of which seeks its peculiar gratification. But all cannot be gratified, for the gratification of one frequently gets in the way of the gratification of another. There is inevitably a certain amount of conflict, of thwarting and frustration. "That organization which is least wasteful of human possibilities is the best."

Poetry represents precisely the record of this "best" organization. "The artist is concerned with the record and perpetuation of the experiences which seem to him most worth having. . . . He is the point at which the growth of the mind shows itself. . . . His work is the ordering of what in most minds is disordered." As we reproduce his experiences, we achieve better co-ordination ourselves, become saner, wiser, and happier. "The basis of morality, as Shelley insisted, is laid not by preachers but by poets."

Mr. Richards's analysis of the relations between science and poetry is very interesting. Both poetry and science deal in "myths," a myth being "a projection of some human situation, of some co-ordination of human feeling, needs, and desires." But there is this difference: we must give unqualified belief to the myths of science, "belief" here meaning not that we think the constructions of science to be objectively and absolutely so, but that we shall always grant them "according action." "What we know as science, that we must act upon, under pain of imminent danger to our lives if we do not." On the contrary, our response in action to the myths of poetry and religion is "restricted and conditional." Poems (and religious beliefs) have served their purpose when they have produced a superior co-ordination of our faculties, an attitude. A single sentence from *Principles of Literary Criticism* gives the entire system in essence:

> "The joy which is so strangely the heart of the experience [of tragedy] is not an indication that 'all's right with the world' or that 'somewhere, somehow, there is Justice': it is an indication that all is right here and now in the nervous system."

Arnold, then, regards poetry as a substitute for dogma. Richards identifies dogma (so far as it has value) with poetry. Tolstoi, while keeping clear from either position, joins with them in assigning to poetry the very highest importance as a moral force, and in evaluating it primarily by its moral influence. Let us now look at two other critics who, while they have no greater respect for traditional dogma, abandon the attempt to bind art to morality.

Benedetto Croce, the great Italian historian, educator, and critic, is the author of a complete philosophical system which is much too vast to be summarized in such a study as this, though it is not easy to comprehend his aesthetic theory without some knowledge of the outlines of the whole Crocean philosophy. According to him, there are four (and only four) fundamental forms of human activity —four aspects of mind: the aesthetic, the logical, the economic, and the ethical. Croce's revolutionary change is that instead of making art the apex of man's powers, he makes it the base. It is the first grade of knowledge, prior to logic, prior to morals. Matter makes its impression on mind. Mind imposes its form on matter, grasps it by direct intuition. These intuitions are completely non-reflective, individual, and particular. The mind *expresses* its intuitions, and that expression is art.

All expression is art, and all art is expression. All language is art; the difference between this essay and *Hamlet* is a quantitative, not a qualitative, difference. We all do constantly what the artist does, but our intuitions lack the coherence and complexity of his. This first grade of knowledge is presupposed in all the other grades but does not presuppose them. Speaking theoretically, it is possible to have an aesthetic without an ethic, but it is not possible to have an ethic without an aesthetic.

Art is the intuitive knowledge of particulars. Logic is conceptual knowledge, or knowledge of the universal. All the stuff upon which it works is furnished by the aesthetic activity. Both these activities are purely theoretical, and as such are not subject to moral judgments. The Practical includes two grades which bear the same relation to each other as the Aesthetic and the Logic: the Economic, which consists of particular actions useful to the individual, and the Ethical, which consists of actions based on universal concepts. The Economic underlies the Ethical, the Logic underlies the Economic, the Aesthetic underlies them all. A good deed is better than a good poem, but without poems there can be no good deeds. One cannot overemphasize in this system the primary and non-moral nature of art. It is ultimately the source of morality, but is not itself moral in any way.

I shall mention one other modern critic, Mr. Max Eastman. He has a fondness for psychology, like Mr. Richards, and like Mr. Richards he has taught college classes, but whereas Mr. Richards can adequately be described as a Cambridge don, one would give a more correct notion of Mr. Eastman by calling him a poet and an essayist of radical political views. His book *The Literary Mind* is one of the most readable and entertaining works on the theory of poetry which has appeared in recent years.

He expresses the view, now becoming somewhat old-fashioned, that the onward march of science is fast destroying the claim of any kind of thought except scientific thought to be denominated knowledge. But he breaks sharply with Mr. Richards in his conception of the respective relations which science and poetry bear to conduct. Poetry in Mr. Richards's system, as we have seen, is made to bear a very heavy practical load: it disciplines us for good deeds. Poetry, Mr. Eastman says, gives us the qualities of things, science indicates their uses. So far as it is "pure," poetry has nothing to do with conduct; it enables us merely to have a "heightened consciousness" of things, to feel them, to live in them. The moment we begin to organize things so as to do something about them, we cease to be aware of them. That activity is precisely science; for conduct, science is all in all.

Mr. Eastman has a pleasant time exposing the pretensions of the critics, professors, theologians, and metaphysicians. They all indulge in "literary loose talk" in an age that has learned the difference between stating a fact and announcing an attitude. Up to about the time of Francis Bacon, literary men thought of themselves as revealers of the truth. The poet was a seer, a divine teacher. Now science has demonstrated its sole right to impart knowledge, and the field of literature is shrinking. Literary men (including all those who indulge in "literary loose talk") are being remorselessly pushed from one line of defense to another. There is no tenable line of defense. The business of the critic is to realize that the poet has nothing to do with the transmission or revelation of truth: he is concerned not with conduct but with experience. He gives us the qualities of things, not their uses. Poetry is an extension of experience, and all experience is valuable for its own sake.

IV

I shall now, I hope with proper humility, point out my objections to these systems. Arnold seems to me an example of a man carrying on by the ethical momentum of a discarded theology. His character was formed by association with his father, the intensely spiritual broad-churchman, Thomas Arnold. Without that background of training and habit he would not have arrived at his own moral earnestness. He did not get it from "culture," nor can anybody else. Secular literature, divorced from theology and dogmatic morality, will not produce it. It would be truer to say that Arnold's moral character, already formed, found partial expression in Homer, Sophocles, and the Bible.

Tolstoi made, as I believe, one contribution of permanent importance to aesthetics: he established for the first time the twofold nature of the critical act. But he substituted his own narrow and fanatical system of dogma (Fatherhood of God, Brotherhood of Man, Vegetarianism, Non-Resistance) for that of the Church. He subscribed to a belief in the natural goodness of man which I think overwhelmingly controverted by fact, and he assigned to art a greater direct power over conduct than I believe it to possess, even when art is as rigorously censored as he demanded.

Richards is a prime example of the "nothing-but fallacy." I have great admiration for his attempt to set up a psychological theory of criticism, and so to reduce one stage, at least, of the critical act to a science. I like his preoccupation with specifically aesthetic problems, and the freedom and elasticity of his literary tastes. With every one else who has considered poetic theory in our days, I have learned a great deal from him. So far as what he has said can be used to defend the autonomy of the aesthetic judgment on naturalistic grounds, I am glad to follow him. But I do not find in my own experience that a purely naturalistic or "psychological" theory of value covers the facts satisfactorily when one leaves the aesthetic judgment; in short, I do not find myself able to accept his naturalistic fusion of morality and aesthetics. I think it is clear that in order to compensate for the loss of religious sanctions he has made poetry carry a heavier burden of moral discipline than it ever, in fact, does carry.

Croce and Eastman are at poles asunder, and I shall not pause to differentiate them. The incompatibility of their systems *as a whole* with any kind of Christian orthodoxy is obvious. But though I am a professional teacher of literature and might be expected to approve of any theory which magnified the importance of poetry, I am more in accord with their fundamental positions than with those of Arnold, Tolstoi, and Richards.

I accept the conclusion that it is not of the essence of art either to reveal truth or to make men better. The artist, *qua* artist, does not show the human mind at its highest stage of development. All attempts to prove good artists to be necessarily good men are transparent sophistries. Poetry expresses mental experiences, some of which, when taken into another mind, may strengthen the moral fiber, while others may corrode it. Whether the moral effect is good or bad is quite immaterial so far as the *aesthetic* judgment of poetry is concerned. Milton, in

Paradise Lost, has handled this problem of the nature of art with great subtlety. The hand of Mulciber, when he fell from heaven, lost none of its cunning; he was just as good an artist in Hell as he had been in Heaven.

"Good" in criticism means two distinct things: "good as art," and "good for you." A man of saintly character who happens also to be endowed with artistic genius, will create (or at least will publish) only works of art of high seriousness, but a man of vicious character may be a very great artist. Works of art are like things which can be eaten or drunk: some of them nourish us, some are downright poisons; some, while totally unnourishing, are pleasant to the taste and do us no appreciable harm. Or works of art can be compared to the living productions of Nature: they may be useful to man, but to be useful to man is no part of the definition of their being. From the point of view of a herpetologist, a good cobra is a full-grown, healthy, typical specimen, with practical fangs and enough poison in his sacs to kill a man. From the point of view of you and me there are no good cobras. The herpetologist's judgment corresponds to the aesthetic judgment, which is the first stage in criticism; your judgment and mine, to the moral evaluation, which is the second.

Men do not become good by refining their mental experiences. They become good by freely submitting their wills to dogmatic imperatives. For that reason poetry cannot take the place of dogma. Mr. T. S. Eliot's judgment of Arnold may also be extended to Richards:

> "Nothing in this world or the next is a substitute for anything else; and if you find that you must do without something, such as religious faith or philosophic

belief, then you must just do without it. I can persuade myself, I find, that some of the things that I can hope to get are better worth having than some of the things I cannot get; or I may hope to alter myself so as to want different things; but I cannot persuade myself that it is the same desires that are satisfied, or that I have in effect the same thing under a different name."

Science is no substitute for dogma, nor is poetry. If you cannot accept dogma for what it purports to be, you will save yourself ultimate trouble by just doing without it. I do not "believe" in the Church on prudential grounds, nor do I cultivate religion as a prop to keep my mind from sprawling. I simply believe, from participating in the Church's life, that its dogmatic pronouncements are *true* —truth supernaturally revealed in accordance with human powers. I believe that science and poetry must be given complete freedom to express the world in their own ways, but that their constructions must finally be evaluated by religion (and for me that means dogma)—not the other way about.

IX

THE MORAL EVALUATION

OF LITERATURE

For some time I have been led to examine the relations between the theories of general linguistic science and literary criticism, and the more I ponder those relations, the more convinced I become that we have here a fresher and surer guide than is to be found in any other philosophical approach. The great virtue of the linguistic approach is that it confines the problem sharply to the art of linguistic expression, and enables one to come to much more specific and practical assumptions than is possible if one insists on principles that are applicable to the whole field of the arts.

The first assumption that I ask you to consider is that literature is merely human speech, and that all specifically aesthetic problems in the field of literature are linguistic problems. When a man composes an elaborate fiction by writing on paper or by using a typewriter, and then has that fiction printed and sold, he is engaged in the same kind of activity as a man who tells a story in a club room or in an after-dinner speech. When a poet, by choice of words, by rhyme and meter, by assonance and alliteration, strives to transmit to unknown readers the tone and quality of some experience, he is doing the same kind of thing that you did yesterday when you tried to convey to your neighbor the enjoyment you had in an afternoon walk. There is a great difference, of course, but it is a difference of degree, not of kind. The poet or novelist is simply doing more skillfully and on a larger scale what we all do after a fashion. Elaborate form (and under this heading I include not merely rhyme, alliteration, meter, and rhythm but also plot or design) does not make poetry, though it does make particular poems: it reinforces, concentrates, and complicates the purely expressive qualities of language so as to produce a product that is more valuable and memorable than the fleeting and atomic poetry of ordinary speech.

We must therefore not confine our thinking to books if we really want to get at the heart of our problem. Books represent only the tiniest fraction of literary art. The art of books is continuous with the art of magazines and newspapers; finally, with the whole expanse of unrecorded speech. The Puritanical censor has far too narrow a view of his task. If he could sweep all printed books out of existence, he would still leave a large, flourishing, and absolutely ubiquitous expanse of literary art, most of it completely beyond the control of public censorship. Critics talk feelingly of "universal art," and imagine that there are great books which appeal to all men of all times. They forget or ignore the fact that throughout human history the majority of mankind have been illiterate, and that of those who can read, the majority have never looked into the books that are supposed to be universal. It is safe to conclude that the one *really* universal kind of literary art is, and to all appearances always has been, smutty stories.

My second assumption is that there is no necessary connection between literary power and moral virtue. When we see a man of extraordinary physical strength or dexterity—say a prize fighter or a champion swimmer—we do not conclude that he is necessarily a good man. We ought to assume exactly the same attitude toward literary artists. The power of expression is one which some men have to an extraordinary degree, but this brilliant power of expression can coexist with a quite ordinary degree of private virtue. We all know this and admit it practically when we say that so-and-so is a scoundrel but a very amusing man, or again when we deprecate frank biographies of poets on the ground that "it is the poetry that matters." The power to express virtue in words is a linguistic or aesthetic power; it implies a knowledge of virtue but not the practical will to do good deeds. The literary artist is a man gifted in one particular direction: he has the gift of speech.

Men in general have rebelled against this conclusion, and have set up definitions of aesthetic value which include moral goodness or "rightness" of subject matter as an essential constituent. Mystical aesthetic (which is usually fathered on Plato but seems to have been the invention of Plotinus) assumes that the poet is a kind of seer, and that the form he imposes on his materials is a reflection of higher reality.

Another theory which is being eloquently developed by Christian apologists in our own day admits that a man can possess literary *talent* of a high order without being morally good (for an artist is a sinner, like every one else) or without having a practical conviction of the truth of a traditional theology, but insists nevertheless that the lack of true belief imposes a definite aesthetic limitation in the product, for without the insight afforded by an adequate "myth" the poet cannot make sense of the experience with which he is dealing. His myth does not so much enable him to *select* images as to *see* them. The aesthetic and ethical judgments are inextricably related, and the judgment from the standpoints of philosophy and theology is primary. A specifically aesthetic judgment is legitimate only when it is recognized as part of a larger evaluation which begins with a consideration of the moral worth of the subject matter.

In spite of the enormous vogue that mystical aesthetic has enjoyed, I am convinced that as general theory it leads to sophistries of little utility. Poets by and large are obviously not superior to other men in either virtue or wisdom unless one redefines morality and wisdom so as to make them so. It is one of the flagrant injustices of history that Plato should be charged with this view, for he expressly repudiated it, and exiled all but a few well-disciplined poets from his ideal commonwealth on the ground that poets as a class are too irresponsible to be tolerated in a wholly reasonable community. Tolstoi in his demand for rigorous religious censorship comes to exactly the same conclusion, though not by the same metaphysical route. It should surely give us pause to find that the two greatest literary geniuses who ever wrote on theory of poetry declined to subscribe to the flattering theory that poets are necessarily seers.

The theory that poetry can have genuine aesthetic value only as it has sound moral content, or, to put it differently, that the images of the poet are vitiated of significance in the extent to which they are not perceived and expressed in the light of a true theology, is much more compelling. I am aware of course of the impossibility in any ultimate sense of separating the form of poetry from its content: when we do separate them, we are only considering the same entity by turns within certain limited and exclusive assumptions. I am also aware of the importance of the beliefs of the poet, not merely in framing and directing his poem, but also in making clear to him what he is trying to express. The last lecture in my Messenger series is an extended demonstration of this principle. Wordsworth's images at the beginning of *Tintern Abbey* are not the full reporting by some unselective machine of all the disturbances a perfectly receptive machine might be supposed to record (the analogy is imperfect, but never mind); they are rather images expressive of the perception of a landscape in terms of a particular religious philosophy. I should not, as a teacher, devote so much time to the study of Wordsworth's thought if I did not think that such study was something more than an evaluation of his doctrines; was, in fact, an aid to the aesthetic appreciation of his poetry. My difficulty is not with the contention that what we conceive to be the soundness or lack of soundness of the poet's beliefs and attitudes will, and should, be a part of our total judgment of his poem; nor is it with the contention that his beliefs and attitudes have the most intimate possible kind of relationship with his images. It is rather with the doctrine that a particular poet with a particular historically limited sensibility will be not only more wise *but also more expressive* in the precise degree to which he subscribes to a right tradition. I should like to believe that, but I find the evidence of history very strongly against it.

History, as I read it, does not support the theory that the relation between expressive power and wisdom is direct and quantitative. Poets not infrequently grow less poetical as they become wiser and more orthodox. I have no doubt that Wordsworth after 1815 had a sounder theology than he had in 1798, and no doubt that he wrote weaker poetry. Mr. T. S. Eliot has reminded us that a poet cannot always write poetry directly expressive of his beliefs. If he wishes to write genuine poetry, he must remain within the limits of his sensibility, and there may be a permanent cleavage between his sensibility and his faith. Consequently, as in Mr. Eliot's own case, his poetry may be a great deal less positive in its statements of belief than his prose. Or, to put it differently, a man can employ for the purpose of poetry only that portion of his beliefs that he can *feel*, the portion that comes to him in terms of quality.

It does not look as though genuine poets start with "myths," with theological and philosophical systems which they proceed to embody in verse. They begin with a sensibility, with an irresistible urgency towards expression which starts them composing before they have much of anything to say. Their search thereafter, so far as they are poets, is not so much for truth and wisdom in an abstract sense as for sanctions for their sensibility, for a body of ideas which will justify their expressive urgency. If they are fortunate as artists (fortunate as *men* is a different matter), they will arrive at just such a body of sanctions as will enable their sensibility to work freely and confidently, and no more. History does not show that unlimited capacity for the poetic absorption of sound belief which this theory demands. It can be maintained that the comparative failure of Wordsworth's later poetry was due more to a waning of natural energy than to the stubborn forcing of an orthodoxy on a historically limited sensibility which could not give poetic body to it, but such evidence as we actually have rather suggests that if Wordsworth had arrived at a complete Christian orthodoxy in 1797 and had insisted on trying to give full expression to it in his poetry, he would have written weaker poetry than he did. His heresies, such as they were, were the necessary condition for the full exploitation of his poetic gift.

Now I know what the reply of the theological critics would be: sin. Cleavage between sensibility and sound belief is, they would assert, evidence of the fallen nature of man. In a state of innocence such a thing could not occur. That is highly theoretical, but it sounds reasonable. If the theological critics will admit that their definition of poetry does not describe the actual poetry of this actual world, but applies only to the poetry of the Garden of Eden, all our differences will be at an end. I think I understand now what Mr. T. S. Eliot meant when he said with reference to Matthew Arnold's dictum that poetry is at bottom a criticism of life, "At bottom: that is a great way down; the bottom is the bottom." He was not, as I thought when I first read the passage, being weakly facetious. He was giving expression to a conviction that a literary history

based on ultimate theological principles is not very rewarding. In the light of eternity and with reference to the day
of judgment there is probably not much that anybody
wants to say about the poetry of William Wordsworth.
But in the light of nature there is a great deal.

My own experience has led me to believe that the fullest
and most satisfactory results can be obtained by applying
both a naturalistic and a theological technique, and by
making the aesthetic judgment wholly within naturalistic
(which means relativistic) assumptions. I find it better to
see linguistic art as something ubiquitous and primary,
something to be judged without fixed moral reference: the
direct expression of the qualities of experience without regard to its uses. This involves a separation of the aesthetic
judgment (whether a thing is good *art*) from the moral
judgment (whether a thing is *good* art).

The position too often taken by those who find the
mystical synthesis unsatisfactory is that of the hedonist, of
"art for art's sake." According to this school, it is profanation of literary criticism so much as to hint the question of morals. This view, which, in modern times at
least, rose as a reaction from strongly moralistic criticism,
errs as much on one side as moralistic criticism does on
the other. Hedonistic criticism is quite right in maintaining that the criticism of literature, as an activity distinct
from other activities of the mind, concerns itself with
aesthetic value and not with moral utility. The critics of
this school have right on their side when they maintain that
the moralistic critic, in his eagerness to answer the question, "Is this good for me?" is ignoring the basic question,
"Is this a powerful work of art?" And to confine our

analysis of things to their practical utility is certainly a narrow and inhumane limitation. It is as though we should restrict our concern with trees to the edibility of their fruit: to say of the yew tree that its berries are poisonous, and dismiss as irrelevant or dangerous any admission that it is beautiful.

But the hedonist errs in forgetting that, as literature is speech, it is the whole of speech, and that as speech has been evolved to express and communicate the whole nature of man, including his moral nature, it is impossible to use speech in such a way that it will have practical meaning without either stating or implying moral concepts. The concept of pure poetry (art whose significance could be exhausted by a strictly aesthetic judgment) is useful and necessary in theory, but no pure poetry exists in practice. Poetry has a special way of saying things, and that way of saying things is what makes it uniquely interesting, but the things it says cannot be held to be empty of moral significance. The dilemma is easily solved if we will agree to maintain both points of view and protect our judgment on the one side from being encroached upon by our judgment on the other. The first of our judgments is purely and specifically literary; the other merges with our other practical decisions.

This being so, we should expect the concept of greatness or supremacy in literature to be in the long run a practical compromise between the claims of the aesthetic and the moral. Common sense prefers two values to one if the two may be had without getting in each other's way. We must sometimes admit that in the perfection of their expressive technique there seems to be little to choose between two given books. But if one of them proceeds from a frivolous, shoddy, or perverse mind and the other from one that is deep, serious, and intense, students of literature (who are merely people who give themselves opportunities to meet literature in its full range) will in the long run find themselves better pleased with the second. But we must repeat again: it was not the moral value of the subject matter which made either book literature in the first place. It was the unusual degree of expressive power possessed by their authors, a power dependent in no certain way on the soundness of their ideas.

I have now granted the reasonableness—indeed, the necessity—of moral judgments in literature, but I do not find myself very well pleased with the history of such judgments. Moralistic criticism of the past too often seems pompous and fussy. It is probable, in the first place, that moralistic critics have reprobated as immoral what was merely revolutionary in technique; and, in the second place, that they were too simple and direct in their conclusions as to the effect of literature on conduct.

I can think of no surer guard against the first error than serious study of the history of language. We are all familiar now with the two views as to "correctness" in speech: on the one hand, the purist view, which maintains the notion of an inherent and absolute correctness in language, fixed by grammars and dictionaries, and sees actual speech as in a deplorable state of decay; on the other hand, the historical view, which regards the statements of grammars and dictionaries as merely descriptive of what has once been the accepted pattern of language for the more elevated forms of discourse. The historical student of language believes that the contemporary vernacular is not in a state of decay but in a state of vigorous and healthy growth. Since language is art and creation, it must change as each individual mind and each society sets itself to express a changing world. This sort of change is neither moral nor immoral, yet it excites more passion than genuine moral turpitude. Most of us can get on quite pleasantly with a libertine, but we hate and despise a man who uses "contact" as a verb. It is a great pity that moral fervor should thus be wasted, and the situation is one that could certainly be improved by better public education in language. It would be better for us to be informed and dispassionate students of the vernacular, eager to observe its variations and novelties, seriously striving to discern the pattern and tone of the emerging idiom. For we can be quite certain that many of those novelties will establish themselves as part of the standard speech which purists of the future will in their turn defend as "correct."

It requires no long historical study of criticism to see that a great deal—I was going to say nine-tenths—of the passionate moral disapproval which has been visited on contemporary literature at all times has really been roused by the style of the work and not by its moral content. It is only human to suspect that innovators are up to no good. It is natural to feel that the world is going to the dogs, and in no way so clearly and certainly as in the arts. But education, if it has any function at all, should aim at training men's minds to distinguish between prejudices; and it is very discouraging to see a large group of men who speak with easy scorn of the critics who failed to discern the greatness of Wordsworth or Keats adopting toward their own contemporaries the attitudes that they condemn in Jeffrey and Lockhart. There is little virtue in recognizing greatness that is already established. The admirable thing is to recognize and describe emerging greatness, even (as will frequently happen) when you cannot bring yourself to care much for it.

Style or expression in itself is not a moral matter. It is to be judged simply and solely for its *adequacy*, its power to record and communicate what the author chose to record and communicate. You cannot decide in advance—you cannot decide, indeed, without prolonged and serious study—that any new departure in style is bad. You must satisfy yourself that you understand what the author wanted to do. If he succeeded in doing that with precision and economy, then he is an artist to be reckoned with. But of course you do not have to give your approval to the subject matter which he chose to express. If it seems to you —again on mature consideration—to be trifling or vicious, your judgment will not be complete until you say so. But do not make the mistake of saying that an author is a bungler when you mean that you find the content of his mind disgusting. A man can be an artist in obscenity and blasphemy no less than in matter of positive moral worth.

The demand that literature shall be moral cannot be narrowed to a demand that it shall explicitly inculcate Christian principles. Literature for a long time now has been overwhelmingly secular, and I do not see how we can expect that it should be anything else. For literature is a sensitive and faithful reflection of the general temper of its age, and the world itself must change before the artist does. Our own age, by and large, is one of moral uncertainty, self-distrust, and violence, and if the artist pictures it so, provided he does it with seriousness and largeness of mind, we ought not to accuse him of depravity. A demand at the present moment for a literature that shall generally avoid coarseness, brutality, and moral deliquescence is a demand for second- and third-rate authors who follow the excellent but outworn formulas of writers of the past.

I shall now, with the diffidence and uncertainty which always accompanies the application of any abstract principle to particular cases, try to illustrate by reference to three important books by modern authors. I do not write the moralistic part with pleasure, because I do not think that I have any special aptitude for it. My standard of morality is that of Christian orthodoxy. It is important to mention this, not that any one who has read me thus far would have any doubt about it, but because I ought to indicate my awareness that the choice of a particular tradition is not inevitable. Within naturalistic assumptions general agreement is ideally possible. All theologies, on the contrary, are a matter of faith, and appear to me to be outside the area in which general agreement can be demanded on logical grounds. The modern world being decidedly divided and pluralistic in its moral systems, many readers of this book will have to take my moral analysis merely as the demonstration of a questionable method. My three books are Somerset Maugham's *Of Human Bondage*, D. H. Lawrence's *Lady Chatterley's Lover*, and Ernest Hemingway's *For Whom the Bell Tolls*. I hope that my reason for choosing each will become apparent as I proceed.

The stylistic novelty of Maugham's book would have

been more obvious if he had published it in 1897, when it was first drafted, instead of in 1915, when it actually appeared. What he realized (and it was a necessary thing for a modern author to realize) was that the reigning style of elaborate and figured prose had become artificial and meretricious. The modern temper demands greater simplicity and austerity, a much closer approximation to the direct, uninvolved order and unpretentious phrasing of colloquial speech. He realized this ideal with a firmness and integrity that cannot be too much admired, but with the tact which must always be the possession of any author who wishes to be popular, not merely to help other writers to be popular. That is, though he made conscious innovations, he did not go so far beyond the linguistic conventions of well-bred mixed society as to rouse suspicion and resentment. It is hard to believe that *Of Human Bondage* ran much risk of rousing misdirected moral judgments by novelties of style. Indeed, the tactfulness of its style probably preserved it from moral criticism that could justly have been made. Lawrence and Hemingway, however, have both suffered from mistaken stylistic criticism, but for rather different reasons.

Lawrence, who was the greatest genius of the three and probably one of the most gifted men of modern times, made a frontal attack on the linguistic taboo which rules that the simple and direct names for certain bodily functions and parts of the body cannot be used publicly; indeed, can hardly be used at all without an impression of obscenity. The taboo was revolting to him as an artist, and it must be admitted that all the circumlocutions for the forbidden words which standard English sanctions are too elegant and self-conscious to satisfy any one with a feeling for honest style. It was revolting to him also as a moralist: he believed that the taboo was a symptom of social ill-health. Consequently he used all the words liberally, with the result of course that he ran foul of censorship, both official and private. The unexpurgated text of his novel is still not too easy to come by.

It may be that I have not pondered deeply enough the moral implications of taboo, but it seems to me that this problem is much less one of morals than it is one of tact and taste. The determination to use subject matter that he did use certainly involved a moral choice, but given that subject matter, Lawrence as an artist had a right to draw on all the resources of language to express it. But if he had not been self-willed and fanatical—in short, if he had had more common sense—he would have seen and admitted that linguistic taboo is far too powerful to be overthrown by a single author, be he ever so gifted. The medium of words has a decorum, like the medium of any other of the arts: there is a great area in which change can be attempted with hope of success, but limits beyond which change—or at any rate sudden change—is impossible. Significant authors are always trying to raise the ordinary homely words of the vernacular to the level of standard English, but this was not the same thing. These words are under some degree of taboo at all levels, not merely in the drawing-room; and because of their immemorial associations of covertness and slyness are not plastic even in the hands of a master of language. What he aimed at was naturalness, but the effect was to make the speech of his characters strained and unnatural. The experiment was a linguistic failure, and so far his book can be condemned on purely aesthetic grounds, though I should of course add that this judgment applies to only one feature of his style, which is uneven but as a whole extremely competent.

The stylistic experimentation of *For Whom the Bell Tolls* is of a particularly massive and resourceful kind. It is much more audacious than Maugham's but much more tactful than Lawrence's. Hemingway is not interested in reshaping the sexual mores of the community. There is nothing defiant in his use of unconventional language. He simply wants to write about people—a band of guerrilla soldiers and a gypsy woman—who naturally and habitually use unconventional language, and he wants to express the actual quality of this speech. He is aided by the fact that all the conversation in the book is supposed to be in Spanish, and that the indecencies are therefore not identical with ours. By thinking the speeches in Spanish and then translating them literally into English (at least by using this technique often enough to give a prevailing cast to the style), he keeps the reader constantly aware of a foreign setting and a foreign mentality whose forbidden words, when seen in print, are not so shocking as ours. Some of the indecencies he can leave in Spanish, but this device must be employed sparingly, for comparatively few of his readers can be expected to be fluent in that language. The foreign words, by and large, must be those which an intelligent English-speaking reader can guess accurately enough from the context or from their similarity to words he does know. But for the great majority of the indecencies he prints the English word *obscenity*, a mere counter which we can accept as such (and most of

the indecencies of vulgar speech are mere counters or ex-
pletives) or convert silently into English coin. The failure
or success of the experiment can be judged only by those
who have read the book carefully and without impatience.
My own conclusion is that it is a successful device but probably a *tour de force*. Hemingway has accomplished something that has hitherto baffled the literary artist, but it is
doubtful whether the device can become generally useful.

It seems to me, then, that any man who professes to care
for literature can read all three of these books with lively
appreciation, analyzing the linguistic problem that faced
each author and estimating the degree of his success in
solving it. We ought to be able to be interested in crafts-
manship considered purely as such. Let us not mistake:
there are great values to be had from the patient and calm
contemplation of linguistic expression without the intrusion
of moral judgment. And those values are the specifically
literary ones; the ones, that is, that distinguish literary
criticism from other activities of the mind.

But there are other values that a serious mind must consider, and other loyalties more important than that to art.
For art (as I have said elsewhere) is experience, and man
as a moral being is surely under the necessity of subjecting *all* his experiences to moral evaluation.

I hope I have indicated sufficiently my admiration for
Mr. Maugham as a literary craftsman. I feel more complete
sympathy with his methods than with those of Lawrence
or Hemingway, because his style is less advanced and
more like what I can imagine myself as being capable of
attaining. I do not find myself in sympathy with his philosophical ideas or the cast of his morality. *Of Human Bond-*

age may well turn out to be the most important English novel of the first quarter of the twentieth century. If it fails of so high a rating, it will be because of its moral shortcomings. It is, if not a deliberately low-principled book, at least one whose principles waver between a facile cynicism and an equally facile sentimentalism. Much of the objection could have been obviated if Mr. Maugham had expressly made all the philosophical and moral speculation that of his hero and had kept himself clear, but he does not do so. The book is tendentious. The direction of its serious purpose is to discredit the Christian religion and the human conscience, but remnants of both are revived at the end for literary effect. I do not object that Maugham has attacked institutional Christianity, for institutional Christianity is fair game; I do object that he has done it with so little candor. *Of Human Bondage* reduces the complex and noble matter of traditional Christian morality to a cold gentlemanly code of selfishness and irresponsibility and then dissolves in a warm bath of benevolence and self-sacrifice which is equally selfish.

It seems to me not too harsh to call Mr. Maugham's moral relaxation ignoble, but no such term can be applied to Lawrence. Lawrence was an intense moralist, a man of tremendous purpose, who sacrificed himself unhesitatingly to an end which he believed good. He was a fanatic and a heretic, trusting in an intense personal intuition rather than a historical tradition. He broke with Christian morality as completely as Maugham, but there is this important difference: Maugham is sensitive to the Christian tradition and is well aware of its reflection in ordinary social morality though his interpretation of its operation is consistently cynical. Lawrence writes as though he were utterly unaware that it existed as anything but a speculative position. For this reason every one of the characters in *Lady Chatterley's Lover* is an animal deviating from the normal type, a monster. There can be no doubt that his mind was pure and that he was filled with passionate tenderness: it was in fact the shamefaced and prurient reticence of traditional writing and speaking about sexual relations that impelled him to write as he did. But he seems to have had no sense of humor whatever, and is consequently always in danger of lapsing into the ridiculous. In matters of style reference to the standards of older authors is unfair, but in matters of morality such reference is legitimate. Put Lawrence's sexual philosophy beside Fielding's and the comparison is very hard on Lawrence. Fielding is virile and robust to the point of coarseness; he is perfectly frank, and his attitude toward sexual license in young men is pretty easygoing. But he has no doubt that such behavior *is* licentious, and his attitude, though stemming fundamentally from his Christian principles, is strongly reinforced by a sense of humor, which is only a sense of proportion. *Fanny Hill* he would have considered just a dirty book which, as a magistrate, he ought perhaps to suppress; if he sent the author to jail it would have been merely to teach him manners. He would not, I think, have considered *Lady Chatterley's Lover* a dirty book, but he would have thought it a ridiculous and possibly a mad book. He would, that is, have seen in it strong signs of obsession and morbidity, and he might have felt it his duty to make inquiries as to whether its author displayed sufficient social responsibility to make it safe to leave him at large. I have, by a fiction, put the onus of this verdict on Fielding's shoulders, but I am willing to assume it myself. It seems to me, as it seems to Mr. T. S. Eliot, that *Lady Chatterley's Lover*, though a remarkable work of art, is the work of a very sick man.

For Whom the Bell Tolls, on the contrary, seems to me in its total effect wholesome and even noble. As I have insisted before, the linguistic audacities must be treated as such, not as moral lapses. In the subject matter to be expressed, Hemingway's grasp of moral principle is large, serious, and patient. The book is remarkably full-blooded and remarkably healthy. Political issues are treated fairly and objectively; if Hemingway is a partisan, it is as a partisan of humanity, to whom the death of every man, whether Loyalist or Fascist, is a loss. The love of Robert Jordan and Maria, though handled with greater intimacy than would have been permitted in the last century, is a relationship of tenderness and responsibility: in the canonical practice that obtained before the Council of Trent it would (I guess) have been rated a clandestine but a valid marriage. I do not see how any one who comes to grips with the story can fail to find positive moral value in it.

As to the others, what shall one say? Is a man necessarily the worse for having read *Of Human Bondage* and *Lady Chatterley's Lover?* It would be much more comfortable to be able to give a direct and categorical answer, but I am not encouraged by history to think that such questions can be answered absolutely. The direct Puritan course of branding all secular literature as not convenient is simply impossible for societies which do not segregate themselves from the world; and the experiment, where it has been tried by secular bodies, cannot be said to commend itself to general acceptance. The Puritan retained the Bible because it was the word of God, but the Bible is a fairly extensive library of books and contains some pretty strong stuff. It is, I suggest, no accident that the Puritan, cut off from secular literature and given a special indulgence as to the Bible, developed a fondness for the harshest and most violent parts of it. His reason was aesthetic (for the violent portions of the Bible, e.g., the minatory Psalms, are especially fine as literature), but the result was moral, and moral in a most unfortunate way. When the ordinary man (I do not speak of saints) restricts his aesthetic experiences, he runs the risk of moral unbalance.

This warns us that the relation between aesthetic experience and moral behavior is by no means so simple as is assumed by the Puritan, whether Christian or humanist. Our moral natures need food to grow on, and the mysterious chemistry of digestion can convert very unlikely substances to good. The analogy might profitably be extended. The Puritans are very like those pure-food fanatics, who having found out that the human body needs proteins, carbohydrates, and fats for its sustenance, drew the direct conclusion that if a man got them pure in concentrated form and ate nothing else, he would be healthier. Now science has discovered the vitamins, substances which are apparently not digested themselves, but whose presence is necessary if the chemistry of digestion is to be complete. Live on pure proteins, carbohydrates, and fats, and you get scurvy, beriberi, pellagra, and rickets. I think I perceive in some of the sternly moralistic critics of my acquaintance a condition of inflamed nerves similar to beriberi, and I conclude that they would profit by more roughage in their diet.

The potential harmfulness of literature is a highly relative matter, and must in the long run be left pretty much to the individual conscience. Modern thinking, in its effort to find a plausible substitute for dogmatic theology, has put upon literature a greater moral burden than it is actually fitted to bear. We place a pathetic trust in the power of good books to make people good, and we assign to works of literature greater power for public evil than is really justified. Moral character is formed by acts, and the direct training of home, church, and society is, in the long run, infinitely more powerful. When a character is still unformed, we are justified in being overcautious, in excluding books which might be unsettling. Those of us who thrive on coarse food must be sympathetic and respectful toward those whose stomachs really are more delicate; we should not taunt them with infirmity, and they should be very slow to set up prohibitions for us. We must be perfectly honest in our reading, alert to recognize and obviate evil as we would in any other kind of experience. But I think the conclusion can be put more directly: we should strive constantly, and by disciplines more active than reading, to make ourselves good men. The Church would do well to worry less about the demoralizing effect of contemporary literature and more about the sincerity, persistence, and competence of its training of the young. To a man of good will, a man of Christian conscience with a habit of self-examination, the problem of reading can be trusted to take care of itself.

NOTES AND REFERENCES

NOTES AND REFERENCES

Page 2

I have developed this philosophy at length in the eighth essay of this series, "Dogma, Science, and Poetry" (pp. 155–87).

Page 5

Messrs. Brooks and Warren, etc.: Cleanth Brooks and R. P. Warren, *Understanding Poetry*, pp. 320–3; E. A. Poe, "The Poetic Principle" (*Selections . . . from . . . Poe*, ed. F. C. Prescott, 1909, p. 231); *Letters of Robert Browning*, ed. T. L. Hood, 1933, p. 49; P. E. More, "James Joyce," in *On Being Human*, 1936, pp. 69, 93; Matthew Arnold, conclusion of "Thomas Gray" in *Essays in Criticism*, Second Series; A. E. Housman, *The Name and Nature of Poetry*, American printing, 1933, p. 13 ff.; Samuel Johnson, "Dryden," in *Lives of the English Poets*; Thomas Gray, letter to West, April 8, 1742; to Beattie, October 2, 1765 (*Correspondence*, ed. Toynbee and Whibley, 1935, i. 192, ii. 896).

Page 6

The Nature of the Physical World: Cambridge University Press, England, 1928. I paraphrase pages 5–21. The direct quotations (used by permission of The Macmillan Company, publishers, New York) on my pages 8 and 9 are from Eddington's pages 10 and 21. Italics in the last sentence quoted are mine.

Page 9

Einstein's illustration was actually given in terms of a stone dropped from the window of a moving railway coach (*Relativity, the Special and General Theory*, trans. R. W. Lawson, New York, 1920, pp. 9–11, conveniently abridged in *The Autobiography of*

Science, ed. F. R. Moulton and J. J. Schifferes, 1945, pp. 526–7). My more striking version is probably not so good as his, for in the longer flight of a bomb the effect of retardation by air resistance is distinctly apparent.

Page 10

A. E. Housman: The quotation is from *The Name and Nature of Poetry*, Cambridge University Press, England, 1933, pp. 13–16, 18–20 of the American printing, and is used by permission of The Macmillan Company, publishers, New York.

Page 13

Pope and his models: In fact, Mr. Housman specifically denies poetical validity to Pope's *genres*, wherever found: "Satire, controversy, and burlesque, to which the eighteenth century was drawn by the character of its genius, and in which its achievement was unrivalled, are forms of art in which high poetry is not at home" (*ibid.*, 16–17).

Housman's subjective test: *ibid.*, pp. 45–6.

Page 16

Percival Stockdale: I quote pp. 66–7 and 125–6, modernizing the punctuation. The idolatrous capitals in the second extract are Stockdale's own.

"On another page": pp. 84–5.

Byron: Letter to John Murray, September 15, 1817 (*Works: Letters and Journals*, ed. Lord Ernle, iv. 169).

Scott: J. G. Lockhart, *Memoirs of the Life of Sir Walter Scott*, end of Ch. 20 (the year 1810). Byron recorded an equally eloquent eulogium of *The Vanity* in his Ravenna Journal, January 9, 1821 (*Works: Letters and Journals*, ed. Lord Ernle, v. 161–2). Byron was in fact a conscious relativist: "Mr. Bowles's title of '*invariable* principles of poetry,' is, perhaps, the most arrogant ever prefixed to a volume. So far are the principles of poetry from being '*invariable*,' that they never were nor ever will be settled. These 'principles' mean nothing more than the predilections of a particular age; and every age has its own, and a different from its predecessor" (*ibid.*, p. 553).

NOTES AND REFERENCES

Page 32

"In poetry each age has a *unique* problem": I am indebted here to a brilliant article by R. G. Collingwood, "The Theory of Historical Cycles," in *Antiquity*, i (December, 1927). 435–46.

Page 35

W. L. Cross: *The Development of the English Novel*, New York: The Macmillan Company, 1899 and later, pp. 138–9.

Page 37

Sir Joshua Reynolds: *Idler* 82, *Seventh Discourse, Third Discourse* (pp. 257, 99, 26 of the edition in The World's Classics).

Page 39

Keats: "Sleep and Poetry," lines 193–9.

Page 46

Jeffrey: The final paragraph of his review of *Poems in Two Volumes*, 1807, is perhaps unsurpassable as a specimen of the method I deplore: "The publication of the volumes before us may ultimately be of service to the good cause of literature. Many a generous rebel, it is said, has been reclaimed to his allegiance by the spectacle of lawless outrage and excess presented in the conduct of the insurgents; and we think there is every reason to hope that the lamentable consequences which have resulted from Mr. Wordsworth's open violation of the established laws of poetry will operate as a wholesome warning to those who might otherwise have been seduced by his example, and be the means of restoring to that antient and venerable code its due honour and authority" (*Edinburgh Review*, xi (October, 1807–January, 1808). 231.

Page 48

"Homer and Virgil are to be our guides": "A Parallel of Poetry and Painting," *Essays of John Dryden*, ed. W. P. Ker, ii. 139. If it were worth the search, one could find the source of this in Rapin or Le Bossu or Rymer.

"Natural diffidence and scepticism": Dryden's own characterization of himself in "Preface to Sylvae," Ker's collection, i. 260.

Page 49

"It is to raise envy to the living to compare them with the dead": The quotation is from "An Essay of Dramatic Poesy," Ker's collection, i. 99. See also a passage earlier in the same essay: "I will grant thus much to Eugenius, that perhaps one of their poets, had he lived in our age, *si foret hoc nostrum fato delapsus in aevum* (as Horace says of Lucilius), he had altered many things; not that they were not as natural before, but that he might accommodate himself to the age he lived in" (*ibid.*, i. 55). It is sad to find the best quotations for our purpose in an early work, written before Dryden had done much reading in French criticism.

"Dryden does not attack the Elizabethans": He does not here, but he does in "Defence of the Epilogue" on the dubious ground that "one age learning from another, the last (if we can suppose an equality of wit in the writers) has the advantage of knowing more and better than the former" (*ibid.*, i. 163).

Page 51

Wordsworth: The italicization of *permanently* and *permanent* is mine, but the emphasis is Wordsworth's. The notion is central to his thinking at all periods; and the word occurs so frequently in his criticism as to constitute a mannerism. In this same preface we are told that in rustic life the passions of men are incorporated with the beautiful and *permanent* forms of nature; their language is a more *permanent* and a far more philosophical language than that which is frequently substituted for it by the poets. The dedication of *Peter Bell* assures us that the poem was held back twenty-one years and carefully revised "to fit it for filling *permanently* a station, however humble, in the literature of our Country." The quotations on this page are from the *Preface* of 1800 (as revised in 1802), the second *Essay upon Epitaphs* (1810), the *Essay Supplementary to the Preface* (1815), and the *Appendix to Lyrical Ballads* (1802). They can be found most conveniently in *Wordsworth's Literary Criticism*, ed. N. C. Smith, pp. 11, 17, 116, 171, 13, 41.

"A moral interest in the main object": Wordsworth is here referring specifically to epitaphs, but he would not have hesitated to make a wider application.

NOTES AND REFERENCES

Page 52

Wordsworth: The quotations on this page are from the *Preface* of 1800 (as revised in 1802); *Essay Supplementary to the Preface* (1815); the second and third *Essays upon Epitaphs* (1810); *Letter to "The Friend"* (1809); the third *Essay upon Epitaphs* (1810); and *Essay Supplementary to the Preface* (1815) (N. C. Smith's collection, pp. 41, 13, 177, 107, 57, 113, 115, 123, 125, 184–5, 186).

Proof "that the nobler sympathies are not alive" in a man: Wordsworth gives his reasons earlier in the paragraph: "In the mind of the truly great and good everything that is of importance is at peace with itself; all is stillness, sweetness, and stable grandeur" (third *Essay upon Epitaphs* [1810], N. C. Smith's collection, p. 124). It will be noticed that Wordsworth has explicitly or implicitly condemned the taste of all the reigns from Elizabeth to the third George.

Page 53

The quotations from Wordsworth on this page are from *Essay Supplementary to the Preface* (1815); the second *Essay upon Epitaphs* (1810); and a letter to John Wilson, June, 1802 (N. C. Smith's collection, pp. 186, 189, 117, 7).

Wordsworth's choice of the four greatest English poets: In "Opinions Expressed in Conversation with His Nephew and Biographer" (N. C. Smith's collection, p. 256).

Page 54

Footnote: Coleridge's acute comment in the eighteenth chapter of *Biographia Literaria* (ed. J. Shawcross, ii. 57 ff.) should be read. He says that Wordsworth takes for granted "rather perhaps too easily" the reader's acquiescence in his praise and blame; points out that the great poets from Homer to Milton abound in that use of epithets to which Wordsworth objects; and even defends the use of Phoebus—though not Gray's line in which Phoebus occurs.

Page 55

Parallels in Wordsworth's later poetry to the line which he condemns in Gray: Professor Cooper's great concordance enables me to select examples containing Gray's very words:

From May-time and the cheerful Dawn
                        ("She was a Phantom," etc., l. 8).
Are cheerful as the rising sun in May
                        ("These times," etc., l. 8).
The cheerful dawn, brightening for me the east
                        ("A little onward," etc., l. 13).
Genial Spring returned
    To clothe the fields with verdure
                        ("When to the attractions," etc., ll. 43–4).
And fields invested with purpureal gleams
                        (*Laodamia*, l. 106).
When all the fields with freshest green were dight.
                        (*Vernal Ode*, l. 2).
And humbler growths as moved with one desire
Put on, to welcome spring, their best attire
                        (*Poor Robin*, ll. 3–4).
Blow winds of autumn!—let your chilling breath
Take the live herbage from the mead, and strip
The shady forest of its green attire
                        (*Excursion*, III. 307–9).
Two of these passages were published in 1807, and appear to have been composed earlier.

Page 56

Rymer and Johnson on Dryden: Rymer selects this passage to prove that English poetry can hold its own against foreign competition. He compares it at length with night scenes in Apollonius Rhodius, Vergil, Tasso, Marino, Chapelain, and Le Moyne, and gives it the palm: "In this description, four lines [he ends his extract with "sleep"] yield greater variety of matter and more choice thoughts than twice the number of any other Language. Here is something more *fortunate* than the boldest fancy has yet reached, and something more *just* than the severest reason has observed. Here are the *flights* of *Statius* and *Marino* temper'd with a more discerning judgment, and the judgment of *Virgil* and *Tasso* animated with a more sprightly Wit. Nothing has been said so expressive and so home in any other language as the first Verse in this description" ("Preface of the Translator" to René Rapin's *Reflections on Aristotle's Treatise of Poesie*, 1674, sig. b.). Johnson's note is on *Macbeth*, II. i. 49–56 ("Now o'er the one half-world Nature seems dead," etc.), and runs as follows: "This image, which is perhaps the most striking that poetry can produce, has been adopted by Dryden. . . . [The] lines, though so well known, I have transcribed, that the contrast between them and this passage of Shakespeare may be more accurately observed. Night is described by two great poets, but one describes a night of guilt, the other of perturbation. In the night of Dryden, all the disturbers of the world are laid asleep; in that of Shakespeare, nothing but sorcery, lust, and murder is awake. He that reads Dryden finds himself lulled with serenity and disposed to solitude and contemplation. He that peruses Shakespeare looks round alarmed and starts to find himself alone. One is the night of a lover, the other of a murderer."

Johnson and Wordsworth: Samuel Johnson, *Life of Pope, ad fin.;* Wordsworth's second *Essay upon Epitaphs* (N. C. Smith's collection, pp. 118–22). Wordsworth's analysis here is unusually detailed and acute.

Page 64

Tolstoi: So far as my own reading goes, I should suppose that it was Tolstoi himself who first made this explicit separation, thus founding modern theory of poetry. *What Is Art?* (first published in 1898) can claim a place, along with Aristotle's *Poetics*, Lessing's *Laokoon*, and Coleridge's *Biographia Literaria*, among the half dozen most important documents in the history of the subject. Tolstoi's critics have allowed his fanatical dogmas for evaluating "subject matter" to overshadow his permanent contributions to general theory.

Page 65

The primitive nature of poetry: This was the revolutionary contribution of Benedetto Croce, first published in 1900, and developed in his *Estetica*, 1902. (English translation by Douglas Ainslie, *Aesthetic as Science of Expression and General Linguistic*, 2nd ed., 1929.)

Page 66

"Some theorists": Croce and Richards in particular. Croce's system allows four, and only four, fundamental aspects of mind. The aesthetic and the logical are held by him to be purely theoretical or contemplative; the economic and the moral to be practical or active. Besides this division into theoretical and practical, there is a cross-division into particular and general. The aesthetic and the economic deal with individual concepts, the logical and the moral with universals. Mr. I. A. Richards insists that the truly scientific is not concerned with action or attitudes, being "simply our most elaborate way of pointing to things." I side with Mr. Max Eastman (see his note, "I. A. Richards' Psychology of Poetry," pp. 297–317 of *The Literary Mind*, 1931).

Page 67

"Language which gives us the immediate *qualities* of experience": Here I draw heavily on Mr. Eastman's book, mentioned in the preceding note, and Mr. John Crowe Ransom's *The World's Body*, 1938. The two systems seem to me mutually convertible, but Mr. Eastman's terminology fits my purpose better than Mr. Ransom's.

Page 68

"Heightened consciousness": a phrase of Miss Edith Sitwell's, popularized by Mr. Eastman.

Max Eastman: The quotation is from *The Literary Mind*, 1931, p. 187, and is used by permission of Charles Scribner's Sons.

Page 69

"*Any* impractical identification," etc.: *ibid.*, p. 188.

Page 71

The definition: If you prefer the terminology of philosophy, here is Mr. Ransom's formulation: "Science gratifies a rational or practical impulse and exhibits the minimum of perception. Art gratifies a perceptual impulse and exhibits the minimum of reason" (*The World's Body*, 1938, p. 130).

Page 72

"A shift in sensibility means ultimately the perception of a different world": For a fuller treatment of this important principle, with documentation, see my essay, "The Power of Memory in

Boswell and Scott," in *Essays on the Eighteenth Century Presented to David Nichol Smith in Honour of His Seventieth Birthday*, 1945.

Page 73

Aristotle: See *Poetics*, I. 6–9; II. 1; VI. 2–3.

Page 77

Edmund Wilson: The article is entitled "The Canons of Poetry," and appeared in the *Atlantic Monthly* for April, 1934 (cliii. 455–62).

Page 83

Effect of Shelley's poetry: After this was written and printed I realized that I was paraphrasing Shelley himself: "[Poetry] awakens and enlarges the mind itself by rendering it the receptacle of a thousand unapprehended combinations of thought" (*Defence of Poetry*).

Wordsworth: *Lines Composed a Few Miles Above Tintern Abbey*, ll. 108–11.

Blake's pregnant remark might be added: "If it were not for the Poetic or Prophetic character the Philosophic & Experimental would soon be at the ratio of all things, & stand still, unable to do other than repeat the same dull round over again" (Conclusion to *There Is No Natural Religion*, First Series).

Page 84

Reference to the individual conscience: It is generally assumed that Roman Catholics are spared this embarrassment of personal decision, but wrongly so. The *Index* lists very few works in *belles lettres*, and of course no strictly contemporary books. Objectionable literature is covered by the blanket canons preceding the list of forbidden books, but in most cases the faithful will have to decide for themselves whether a given book is "openly hostile to religion and morality" or whether it "openly deals with, or describes, or teaches lascivious or obscene matters."

St. Augustine: "Semel ergo breve praeceptum tibi praecipitur, Dilige, et quod vis fac: sive taceas, dilectione taceas; sive clames, dilectione clames; sive emendes, dilectione emendes; sive parcas, dilectione parcas: radix sit intus dilectionis, non potest de ista radice nisi bonum existere." (Commentary on I John 4. 4–11; Migne's *Patrologia Latina*, 35. 2033.)

Page 87

"The total critical act of evaluation is a compromise": See Matthew Arnold's essay on Byron (*Essays in Criticism*, Second Series) for a masterly development and illustration of this principle.

Page 89

Eastman: See *The Literary Mind*, 1931, especially the second and fourth chapters of the Third Part ("The Tendency Toward Pure Poetry" and "Division of Labor in Literature").

Page 90

Ransom: In *The World's Body*, 1938, pp. 63–75.

Page 91

Coleridge: *Biographia Literaria*, Ch. XIV (ed. J. Shawcross, ii. 11).

Poe: The quoted bits on this page and the following are from "The Philosophy of Composition," "The Poetic Principle," "Review of Bulwer's *Night and Morning*," and "Longfellow's Ballads." They can be found most conveniently in *Selections from the Critical Writings of Edgar Allan Poe*, ed. F. C. Prescott, 1909, pp. 153, 228, 229, 312, 74, 155.

Page 92

George Moore: See *An Anthology of Pure Poetry*, ed. George Moore, New York, 1925, pp. 17, 18, 35.

Page 93

Eastman: *The Literary Mind*, 1931, p. 86.

Page 95

"The justification of such abbreviation of method": The quotation is from T. S. Eliot's preface to his translation of St. John Perse's [i.e., A.-St.-L. Léger's] *Anabasis*, 1930, p. 8.

NOTES AND REFERENCES

Page 97

Ash Wednesday: From *Collected Poems of T. S. Eliot,* copyright 1936, by Harcourt, Brace and Company, Inc.

The commentary on *Ash Wednesday:* I am deeply indebted to Mr. Leonard Unger's article, "Notes on *Ash Wednesday,*" *Southern Review,* iv (Spring, 1939). 745-70.

Page 105

Byron: Goethe's remark is recorded by Eckermann, February 24, 1825 (J. W. von Goethe, *Gespräche,* heraus. von F. von Biedermann, 1910, iii. 164).

Page 109

Publication of *An Evening Walk:* I believe the date has not previously been fixed. I owe the information to the kindness of Mr. James R. Baird, who discovered Johnson's advertisement in the *Morning Herald* for February 6, 1793.

Page 110

"Spots of time": *The Prelude,* XII. 208.

The extended quotation is also from *The Prelude,* IV. 330-44 (text of 1805).

Page 111

"Says Wordsworth": In *The Prelude,* IV. 101-8 (text of 1805).

Page 112

The date of the earliest existing drafts of *An Evening Walk:* My reasons for assigning these to 1792 are as follows: (1) They are so close in style to *Descriptive Sketches* and the published *Evening Walk.* One would expect to find more difference between Wordsworth's writing of 1788 or 1789 and that of 1792. (2) They contain the description of the cock (ll. 129-38), which is closely imitated from P.-F. Rosset's *L'Agriculture,* a book which Wordsworth is more likely to have read after he went to France in 1791 than before. (3) They contain, fully elaborated, the pathetic episode of the female vagrant and her two small children, frozen to death in the storm. The revisions of 1794, now first published by Mr. de

Selincourt, contain a note connecting this passage with the "catastrophe of a poor woman who was found dead on Stanemoor two years ago." Wordsworth is very careless and inaccurate in dates, but it does not seem likely that his "two" was really five or six. In a letter to me dated January 9, 1942, Mr. de Selincourt agreed that the difficulties were best met by assigning the drafts to the period of Wordsworth's residence in France. I regret that I did not have the benefit of his judgment on the hypothesis I now advance, namely that these were the *first* drafts of the poem we know as *An Evening Walk*. This was suggested to me recently (1944) by the Reverend Chester A. Soleta, O.C.S.

Wordsworth's own references in later life are, as usual, confusing. In the Fenwick note to "Extract from the Conclusion of a Poem Composed in Anticipation of Leaving School" he speaks as though *The Vale of Esthwaite* was written in 1786 and was distinct from *An Evening Walk*, but in the note to *An Evening Walk* he says that that poem was written "at school, and during my first two College vacations": i.e., he is equating the two, for it is not likely that he was handling the same material in two verse forms at the same time. There are three MSS for *The Vale of Esthwaite*, one of which is headed by Wordsworth, "Various Extracts from *The Vale of Esthwaite*, a Poem, written at Hawkshead in the Spring and Summer 1787," and the poem contains at least one passage (ll. 529–36, see Mr. de Selincourt's note) which could not have been written before the summer of that year. The juvenile octosyllabic fragment, *The Dog, an Idyllium* (Mr. de Selincourt's edition, p. 264), which contains a reference to Wordsworth's excursions with the dog and an account of his caressing the animal as

> Some new-created image rose
> In full-grown beauty at its birth
> Lovely as Venus from the sea

has an important bearing on the question, but a discussion of it would be too complicated for this note. The simplest explanation of the evidence thus far presented is that Wordsworth began the octosyllabic poem in 1787 while he was at school at Hawkshead; that he went on adding to it in 1788 and 1789, his drafts meanwhile becoming (like the MSS of what became *The Prelude* and *The Excursion*) a collection of disjointed fragments, the later of which

224

he may already have thought of as a new poem; that he then in 1792 recast portions of it in heroic couplets as *An Evening Walk*.

Page 114

M. Legouis: See Émile Legouis, *The Early Life of William Wordsworth*, trans. J. W. Matthews, pp. 133–5.

Page 115

"A form discover'd," etc.: The quotation is from *An Evening Walk*, 1793, ll. 45–8. (The text of 1793 may be found in the one-volume Oxford Wordsworth, as well as in Mr. de Selincourt's edition.) I could have made the passage still harder by leaving the third line as Wordsworth printed it, viz., "The ray the cot of morning trav'ling nigh," but I agree with Mr. de Selincourt that this must have been a misprint.

"The boy no doubt was a 'spot' ": I doubt whether the image is very precise. If Wordsworth knew that the boy was fishing, he presumably could distinguish the fishing-rod. If so, "spot" seems too blurred and indefinite.

Page 116

"When, in the south," etc.: *An Evening Walk*, ll. 53–70, with some emendation of the punctuation from Wordsworth's final text. The punctuation of 1793 puts the schoolboys, not the deer, round the humming elm. (In several other cases I have emended the punctuation of my extracts, but this is the only one that needs to be reported.) This passage illustrates all the faults already enumerated except that of excessive or bizarre personification. (1) *Ellipsis:* "gazing" for "gazing at." (But Wordsworth had precedent; the Oxford Dictionary lists parallel examples from Daniel, Drayton, and Milton.) (2) *Inversion:* "Gazing the tempting shades to them deny'd When stood the shorten'd herds among the tide" in prose order and diction would be, "When the crowded cattle stood in the water, gazing at the tempting shade denied to them." (3) *Poetic diction:* "tide," "flood," "swain." (4) *Obscurity.* Why does the elm hum? The revision of 1794 is a little more explicit:

> A spotted surface, glimmering all alive
> Beneath the Elm that sounded like a hive,

but it is not until we read passages in others of Wordsworth's poems which embody the same observation that we can be sure that we know what he means. The best is *The Excursion*, I. 590–6:

> At this the Wanderer paused;
> And looking up to those enormous elms,
> He said, " 'Tis now the hour of deepest noon.
> At this still season of repose and peace,
> This hour when all things which are not at rest
> Are cheerful, while this multitude of flies
> With tuneful hum is filling all the air" . . .

The flies, like the deer, have come in under the elm to escape the glare of noonday. (English elms have denser shade than ours.) They "trouble" the deer, who keep them in constant motion by restless movements of their tails and their heads. In the final revision the elm became a "broad-spread oak" and the humming ceased.

Pages 117–19

Contemporary criticism of *An Evening Walk:* The references are, in order, Wordsworth's letter to Miss Taylor, April 9, 1801 (*Early Letters*, ed. De Selincourt, p. 270); Coleridge's note on the phrase "green radiance" in "Lines Written at Shurton Bars," *Poems on Various Subjects*, 1796, p. 185; *Biographia Literaria*, ed. J. Shaw-cross, i. 56, 58. See Mr. de Selincourt's notes, pp. 320, 322 of his edition of the *Early Poems*.

Pages 122–3

Windsor Forest: The quoted passages are ll. 98, 126, 194, 21–8, 67–72, 141–6, 211–18.

Page 125

"A smart simile":

> As some coy nymph her lover's warm address
> Nor quite indulges, nor can quite repress.

Page 127

The early critics: The material is conveniently collected in the first volume of Pope's works edited by Whitwell Elwin and W. J. Courthope, p. 321 ff.

Page 130

Delille, Rosset, Roucher, and Saint-Lambert: See *Wordsworth: Representative Poems*, ed. Arthur Beatty, pp. xxxvi, 11, 31–3. This is the most fully and usefully edited Wordsworth we now have. It is a pity that the purposes of the edition did not permit Professor Beatty to include the entire text.

Page 132

"The consecrated formulas": See *Wordsworth: Representative Poems*, pp. 10–11.

Page 134

"Five years have past," etc.; *Lines Composed a Few Miles Above Tintern Abbey*, ll. 1–8, 88–102, Wordsworth's final text. The text of 1798 differs in but three words: *sweet* for *soft* in line 4, *which* for *that* in line 6, and *Not* for *Nor* in line 13 (of my extract).

Pages 138–9

-līc and *līce:* I have simplified in the interests of perspicuity, but I believe I have not misstated the general principles. *Slāwlīc*, "slowly" (adjective) has apparently never existed, and *slāwe*, "slow" (adverb) is not recorded for Old English, which appears regularly to have used *slāwlīce*. Our "slow" (adverb) is recorded only from 1500, and was therefore probably formed from the adjective on the analogy of other adverbs without termination, especially "fast." By the way, do purists condemn compounds like "slow-burning"? If not, why not?

Page 140

"Whom": "The man I saw" and "The man that I saw" are acceptable for all levels of style. "The man who I saw" is colloquial, but is not limited to Vulgar English. See C. C. Fries, *American English Grammar*, 1940, pp. 93–6.

NOTES AND REFERENCES

Page 142

Chaucer's inflection of adjectives may be illustrated by the following four lines from the Prologue to the *Canterbury Tales*: "With hym ther was his sone, a yong [*strong, sing.*] squier"; "The tendre croppes, and the yonge [*weak, sing.*] sonne"; "And I seyde his opinion was good" [*strong, sing.*]; "His hors were goode [*strong, plural*], but he was nat gay." The weak plural was the same as the strong plural.

Page 143

"The early seventeenth century": I mean of course in formal or literary English. In the vernacular, "you" began to be used for "ye" at least as early as the fourteenth century. Shakespeare's plays, which are much closer to contemporary speech than the deliberately archaic style of the revisers of the King James Bible, show "you" and "ye" used interchangeably, "you" being the commoner form.

H. C. Wyld: *Elementary Lessons in English Grammar*, 1925, p. 11. (Quoted from C. C. Fries, *American English Grammar*, 1940.)

Page 147

Archbishop Trench: Richard Chenevix Trench, *On the Study of Words*, Lecture I. "Man starts with language as God's perfect gift, which he only impairs and forfeits by sloth and sin, according to the same law which holds good in respect of each other of the gifts of heaven" (*ibid.*)

Page 153

"Say neither," etc.: Stephen Vincent Benét, *John Brown's Body*, concluding lines.

Pages 156–9

The analysis of the four meanings of the term "Nature" owes a great deal to Mr. I. A. Richards, *Coleridge on Imagination*, pp. 157–8.

NOTES AND REFERENCES

Page 158

"It has no room for the individual": For example, the science of actuarial statistics enables a life-insurance company to assign a predicted life span to me at any age, and to insure me for such an annual premium as will enable the company *in its transactions as a whole* to make a profit. But this gives me no assurance that I shall live ten days or even ten minutes after I have completed the policy.

Page 163

Seneca: See also Plotinus: "For who that is strong enough to meditate upon the original turns by choice to its phantasm? Witness the circumstance that among children it is the dunces who betake themselves to the crafts and manual employments, because they are not competent to learning and meditation" (*Enn.* III. viii. 4, trans. E. R. Dodds).

Page 166

"[Euclidean] geometry sets out from certain conceptions such as 'plane,' 'point,' and 'straight line,' with which we are able to associate more or less definite ideas, and from certain simple propositions (axioms) which, in virtue of these ideas, we are inclined to accept as 'true.' Then, on the basis of a logical process, the justification of which we feel ourselves compelled to admit, all remaining propositions are shown to follow from these axioms, i.e. they are proven. A proposition is then correct ('true') when it has been derived in the recognized manner from the axioms. The question of the 'truth' of the individual geometrical propositions is thus reduced to one of the 'truth' of the axioms. Now it has long been known that the last question is not only unanswerable by the methods of geometry, but that it is in itself entirely without meaning. We cannot ask whether it is true that only one straight line goes through two points. We can only say that Euclidean geometry deals with things called 'straight lines,' to each of which is ascribed the property of being uniquely determined by two points situated on it" (Albert Einstein, *Relativity*, trans. R. W. Lawson, New York, 1920, pp. 1–2, quoted by permission of Peter Smith). He goes on to say that the concept "true" ought not to be applied to abstract systems like geometry, which are free inventions of the human mind; we should demand only that they have logical unity. When the propositions of geometry are applied to the objects of experience ("nature"), we are then justified in asking whether they are "true": i.e. whether they "are satisfied for those real things we have associated with the geometrical ideas" (p. 4).

Page 168

Einstein: *The Evolution of Physics*, by Albert Einstein and Leopold Infeld, 1938 and later, pp. 295–310. Quantum physics gives up all attempt to describe individual cases as objective happenings in space and time, and presents directly the statistical laws governing the motion of a "crowd of individuals behaving in an unpredictable way." This appears to be an admission that physical reality is not entirely comprehensible. My exposition of the conflict between the two theories of the nature of light is drawn from other sections of this remarkable book, pp. 97–104, 110–20, 272–80.

Page 169

The illustration of the jigsaw puzzle: A much better analogy is given by Arthur Koestler in his novel, *Arrival and Departure*. I only wish I had thought of it myself: "As children we used to be given a curious kind of puzzle to play with. It was a paper with a tangle of very thin blue and red lines. If you just looked at it you couldn't make out anything. But if you covered it with a piece of transparent red tissue-paper, the red lines of the drawing disappeared and the blue lines formed a picture—it was a clown in a circus holding a hoop and a little dog jumping through it. And if you covered the same drawing with blue tissue-paper, a roaring lion appeared chasing the clown across the ring. You can do the same thing with every mortal, living or dead. You can look at him through [the red] tissue-paper and write a biography of Napoleon in terms of his pituitary gland, as has been done; the fact that he incidentally conquered Europe will appear as a mere symptom of the activities of those two tiny lobes, the size of a pea. You can explain the message of the Prophets as epileptical foam and the Sistine Madonna as the projection of an incestuous dream. The method is correct and the picture in itself complete. But beware of the arrogant error of believing that it is the only one. The picture you get through the blue tissue-paper will be no less true and complete. The clown and the lion are both there, interwoven in the same pattern. But perhaps I exaggerate when I say that both are equally complete. Since the Renaissance, the red tissue-paper of our scientific reasoning has obtained greater perfection than the blue of our intuition and ethical beliefs. . . . For the last four centuries the first has improved, the second decayed. But prior to that, in the Gothic age, the scales moved the opposite way; and I believe that this process will soon be reversed again." (*Arrival and Departure*, The Macmillan Company, 1943, pp. 177–8, quoted by permission of the publishers. The passage was brought to my attention by Canon B. I. Bell's *God Is Not Dead*.)

Page 176

Arnold: The quotations are from *God and the Bible*, New York, 1875, pp. 104–5 (Chapter II), and the opening paragraph of "The Study of Poetry," which leads off the *Essays in Criticism*, Second Series.

Page 178

Tolstoi: *What Is Art?* Chapter V.

Goodness of art according to subject matter: Tolstoi by no means evades the demand for illustration. Schiller's *Robbers*; Hugo's *Les Pauvres Gens* and *Les Misérables*; Dickens's *Tale of Two Cities*, *Christmas Carol*, *The Chimes*, and others; Harriet Beecher Stowe's *Uncle Tom's Cabin*; Dostoievsky's works generally; George Eliot's *Adam Bede*—are good art. Of his own works he thought all bad except *God Sees the Truth* and *The Prisoner of the Caucasus*. The quotations are from *What Is Art?* Chapters XVI and XX.

Pages 179–80

Richards: The quotations are from *The Principles of Literary Criticism*, 1930, pp. 52, 61, 62, 246. His analysis of the relations between science and poetry is abstracted from one of his later books, *Coleridge on Imagination*, pp. 173–5. In the preface to this volume, he says that he is conscious of having adopted no position at variance with that announced in his earlier works. It seems to me that a significant shift of ground occurs between *Coleridge on*

Imagination and the early *Science and Poetry,* and that I should not be treating Mr. Richards fairly if I took the scheme from *Science and Poetry,* as for many reasons I should like to do.

Page 182

"Both these activities are purely theoretical": Not so simple as it sounds, for with Croce expression is a purely mental event. Every work of art is complete in the mind. Externalizing art by tones, pigments, letters, etc., is not an aesthetic but a practical activity. In publishing a poem a man may become subject to moral censure. It may be necessary to restrict or prohibit the circulation of certain books, but in doing so we may be in the position of having to say, "This is a superb work of art."

"Not itself moral in any way": Croce's system, as will be seen, has no place for religion, which he regards as imperfect philosophy.

Page 183

"It disciplines us for good deeds": Remembering always that Mr. Richards's theory of morals is purely prudential.

Page 186

Milton and Mulciber: *Paradise Lost,* Book I, the building of Pandemonium. See also Book II, lines 552–5, the heroic poetry of the fallen angels:

> Their song was partial, but the harmony
> (What could it less when spirits immortal sing?)
> Suspended Hell, and took with ravishment
> The thronging audience.

"Partial" here means "biassed, unduly favoring themselves," not "imperfect, because they have lost their hold on the divine source of poetic truth" (Hanford). Milton is saying as clearly as he can that poetry can be beautiful without being true.

Eliot on Arnold: Reprinted by permission of the publishers from T. S. Eliot, *The Use of Poetry and the Use of Criticism,* Cambridge, Mass.: Harvard University Press, 1933, p. 106. See also "Arnold and Pater" in *Selected Essays.*

232

NOTES AND REFERENCES

Page 191

Criticism and theology: See especially S. L. Bethell, *The Literary Outlook*, 1943 (The Christian News-Letter Books, No. 17); "Poetry and Theology" by the same author, *Christendom* (British), xiii (December, 1943); "The Relation of Theology to Literary Criticism" by R. W. Battenhouse, *Journal of Bible and Religion*, xiii (February, 1945). 16–22. Mr. Bethell's book is mainly applied criticism of the sort that I should call "criticism of moral judgment." His theory concerning the relations between the artist's sensibility and the effective literary use of his beliefs is not clearly and fully worked out in one place, but consists of a too sweeping general statement preceded and followed by qualifications that are likely to be overlooked. If the qualifications were all collected and the theory rewritten so as to give them proper emphasis, I do not know that there would be a formal difference between our positions. In his practical criticism he sometimes (as it seems to me) steps over the line he says he will not cross and implies that an author's expressive gift the thing which is to be assumed before theological criticism starts) is actually dependent for its existence on sound belief.

Page 194

Eliot: *After Strange Gods*, 1934, p. 30. Dr. Johnson defended this same position again and again and illustrated it by *The Vanity of Human Wishes*. Though as Christian and orthodox as one could wish, he found a paraphrase of Juvenal as positive a poetical expression of his religious feelings as he could manage.

Page 195

Wordsworth: T. S. Eliot has said something similar to this: "I do not take orthodoxy to mean that there is a narrow path laid down for every writer to follow. Even in the stricter discipline of the Church, we hardly expect every theologian to succeed in being orthodox in every particular, for it is not a sum of theologians, but the Church itself, in which orthodoxy resides. In my sense of the term, perfect orthodoxy in the individual artist is not always necessary, or even desirable. In many instances it is possible that an indulgence of eccentricities is the condition of a man's saying anything at all. It is impossible to separate the 'poetry' in *Paradise Lost* from the peculiar doctrines that it enshrines; it means very little to assert that if Milton had held more normal doctrines he would have written a better poem; as a work of literature, we take it as we find it: but we can certainly enjoy the poetry and yet be fully aware of the intellectual and moral aberrations of the author" (*After Strange Gods*, copyright 1934, by Harcourt, Brace and Company, Inc., pp. 34-5).

Eliot: "At the bottom of the abyss is what few ever see, and what those cannot bear to look at for long; and it is not a 'criticism of life.' If we mean life as a whole—not that Arnold ever saw life as a whole—from top to bottom, can anything that we can say of it ultimately, of that awful mystery, be called criticism? We bring back very little from our rare descents, and that is not criticism" (reprinted by permission of the publishers from T. S. Eliot, *The Use of Poetry and the Use of Criticism*, Cambridge, Mass.: Harvard University Press, 1933, p. 103).

Page 208

Eliot: *After Strange Gods*, copyright 1934, by Harcourt, Brace and Company, Inc., pp. 38-9, 62-6.

MIDLAND BOOKS

INDIANA UNIVERSITY PRESS
Bloomington